"*Easy Marriage* is a gem. As a renowneu ....
Dr. Friedin provides a gift to all with this plain- speaking guiu.
to making marriages really work well. He provides much insight
from his many years of experience and offers extensive practical
advice to those getting married for the first or even the third time.
Easy Marriage is timely and filled with both wit and wisdom.
It is very easy to read and it highlights the main points of avoiding the problems that interfere with healthy and positive relationships. Thank you, Dr. Friedin, for taking the time to write such a
poignant and highly accessible book that points to the sustenance
of marriage."

—Gerald D. Oster, Ph.D.
Author, *Unmasking Childhood Depression,*
Life As a Psychologist
and
Helping Your Depressed Teenager
Olney, Maryland

"Insightful, comprehensive and humorous are just a few of the words that will come to mind when one digests Dr. Friedin's straightforward suggestions for marital success. *Easy Marriage* is a must read for couples who are experiencing marital discord and for those who want to improve their relationship. The wide range of information and wisdom is especially formulated for the yet–to-be married singles or couples who will appreciate the advice for the likelihood of an easy marriage."

—Enrico Mango, M.D.
Long Island, New York

Easy Marriage

Easy Marriage

EXPERT ADVICE FOR COUPLES AND SINGLES

—⁓⁓⁓—

Bruce Friedin, Ph.D.

ISBN-13: 9781540411693
ISBN-10: 1540411699
Library of Congress Control Number: 2016920313
CreateSpace Independent Publishing Platform
North Charleston, South Carolina

1.Marriage. 2.Marriage counseling. 3.Sex-Sexuality.
4.Relationships. 5.Divorce. I. Title

Printed by CreateSpace, An Amazon.com Company • CreateSpace, Charleston South Carolina

Available from Amazon.com and other retail outlets, online stores, and other book stores.

Printed in the United States of America

To my wife Ronnie,
my son Dr. Alex Friedin,
my daughter Dr. Jillian Howard
and my son-in-law Daniel Howard, Esq.
With deepest gratitude for your love and inspiration.

This book is like a story I had to eventually tell.
For well over five years, I've either been writing this story
or staring out a window thinking about it.

I want sex that drives me crazy
and conversation that drives me sane.
— Steve Maraboli

Contents

Foreword

—⟋⟍—

Easy is defined as without effort or difficulty. Synonyms include: painless, trouble-free, manageable, undemanding, natural, content, comfortable, calm, tranquil and peaceful.

Difficult is defined as requiring much effort. Synonyms for difficult include: strenuous, demanding, grueling, exhausting, back-breaking, heavy and laborious.

Whether you're dating, engaged, married or living together, Easy Marriage was especially composed for you. If you're about to get married for the second or third time, this book was also composed for you.

Easy Marriage has been years in the making. It's been a passionate venture for me while I've maintained a large practice as a New York psychologist. For a very long time, my specialties have been marital problems and all aspects of sexuality. I know how marriages can start out easy and stay easy. I also know how marriages can transform from horribly difficult to easy.

Easy Marriage is structured into dozens of chapters on the numerous aspects of marriage. Each chapter is brief and replete with suggestions pertaining to the desirability and logic of an easy marriage.

Marriage can absolutely and unequivocally be easy. It's just that most people don't know how to have it.

Preface

—〰—

Men live by forgetting.
Women live by memories.
T.S. ELIOT

I BEGIN THIS BOOK WITH the recommendation that one should *not* believe the advice: "In order to have a good marriage, you have to work at it." This dreary adage has been around forever. Simply put, don't believe it.

In the 1960s when I was a teenager, I was baffled and horrified by this supposed scientific doctrine of truth about marriage. I precociously believed that if a husband and wife are always *working* on their marriage, they shouldn't have gotten married. I believed that a marriage which required constant labor was unappealing and not worth having. But what did I know? I was just a cynical kid.

As a skeptical teenager, certain questions were unavoidable. Why would anyone want to get married if they had to work on their marriage constantly? Is that what marriage is—heavy labor? Then why get married? Why would anyone stay in or want a labor-intensive marriage?

So now over five decades have passed, and my beliefs haven't changed. More than ever, I adamantly believe that you don't have to constantly work on a marriage in order to have a good marriage. Furthermore, you *shouldn't* have to always work on your marriage.

I hold many specific and strong beliefs about good and bad marriages. I should point out that I have five academic degrees, including three graduate degrees and over forty years of professional psychological work.

I've helped people from all walks of life with every conceivable type of psychological, sexual, romantic, and relationship problem you can think of—some of which you can't imagine or didn't even know existed.

Decade after decade, I've asserted that if you are always working on your marriage, either: (A) you married the wrong person; (B) you'd have the same problems no matter whom you married; and/ or (C) you don't have the skills and awareness as to how to have an easy marriage.

I'll be crystal clear: A good marriage doesn't require constant work.

Naturally, married couples enter into therapy with a focus on eliminating problems. But couples don't foresee the bigger picture that eliminating problems makes their marriage more enjoyable *because* it's also making their marriage easier.

Easy Marriage is an easy guide of easy ideas and easy advice which can be easily implemented in order to have an enjoyable and sustainable marriage.

People can learn to make better choices as to whom to marry. And people can have a better life with the person they did marry—if only they were guided in the right directions.

Easy Marriage is straightforward. There are no long-winded, grim descriptions of miserable marriages and no long-winded, sappy passages of how couples should massage each other in candlelit bliss.

This is a practical guide for people who are either married or considering marriage. Just about every paragraph in Easy Marriage offers a useful idea, an insight, practical advice, and thought-provoking quotes.

But what's with the funny quotes, you may ask. Isn't this a serious book about marital problems? Actually, it's *not* a book about marital problems. Rather, it's a book about *avoiding* marital problems.

I've always been a firm believer that humorists such as writers and comedians can make us think, feel and remember at the same time. I believe that many humorists are essentially great philosophers and observers of people. Sometimes, a simple quote can change a person's view on an aspect of life.

A good marriage is an easy marriage. And an easy marriage in-sures a good and lasting marriage. You'll know you have it when you and your spouse feel very fortunate to have each other.

No one book can cover every aspect and nuance of marriage. <u>Easy Marriage</u> offers advice and opinions about some of the most im-portant elements of marriage and the most common issues and conflicts. Again, it doesn't try to cover everything.

I have no doubt that some readers will sneer at my suggestions and concepts, claiming they're simplistic, outdated or unrealistic. Just keep in mind that *your* beliefs are based on your personal experiences; my beliefs are based on decades of helping people in highly painful marriages.

Do any of the following statements sound appealing and relevant in your life:

* The travel directions are easy.
* The parking is easy.
* The instructions are easy.
* The course was easy.
* The recipe is easy.
* Getting there is easy.
* The rules are easy.
* Easy to work with.
* Fixing it was easy.

So, do you prefer a difficult marriage or an easy marriage?

Introduction

—ɯɯ—

One day your life will flash before your eyes.
Make sure it's worth watching.
?

MARRIAGE IS NOT FOR EVERYONE. And marriage is certainly not the only pathway to happiness in life. Just as a college education or having children are not automatic pathways to happiness, neither is marriage. The world is filled with content single people and miserable married people.

It seems as if philosophers and noteworthy thinkers over the centuries come from the same mold that everything worthwhile in life requires work and involves difficulty. That nothing comes easy in life. Just work and difficulty for reaching any kind of worthwhile goal.

Well, I cannot argue that some things in life require work and involve great amounts of labor, but this type of thinking doesn't apply to marriage.

The pressure to marry is complex. For various reasons, divorced people—especially women—feel *adequate* as long as they've been married once (or more). This is compared to single women who view themselves as *inadequate* because they were never married even once.

It's sad and completely unwarranted that some people are ashamed because they were never married. Being single doesn't make one defective!

Where and when was it ever determined that a person is a failure if they're not married? Or that a person is a failure if they're divorced? How sad and undeserved that some people define themselves as inadequate if they never married.

Unfortunately, this is exactly what prompts some people to marry prematurely. In other words, they settle out of desperation. Their marriage then becomes destined to be painful and problematic, leading to a dark ending either in divorce or eternal marital misery.

Here's a perspective on marriage and divorce: about half of all first marriages end in divorce. And the rate is higher for second marriages. Of the remaining marriages, a large percentage would end in divorce if it wasn't for three factors: children, a comfortable home and finances.

Obviously as a society, we're not very good at marriage. The divorce rate would be even much higher if divorce was easier and less costly.

I unequivocally believe that across generations, we are not teaching our children how to get into good marriages nor how to have a good married life. Yet we know how to give weddings and wedding showers. But it doesn't have to be this way.

It is pathetic and disgusting how vicious and ruthless some people are in their divorce process. It is disgraceful how some spouses turn their children against the other parent; and most of the time, it's only about money. Obviously, it isn't much of a stretch to predict that if your marriage is difficult, your divorce will be excruciating.

Some miserable, angry people treat their spouses and marriages poorly, but they have little insight about their own obnoxious personality problems and their lack of interest in having a good marriage. Chances are no one else would have an enjoyable marriage with this person either. Such people won't even benefit from marriage counseling.

Some people are just not meant to be happily married. They are never content. They can't make themselves happy, and they can't or won't try to make their spouse happy.

All marriages will have various struggles from time to time. There are no marriages without problems. But in good marriages, however, many problems are prevented and many problems are resolved well.

Some people realize too late that they married the wrong person. Unfortunately, nothing will fix their problems and their marriage. No intervention will fix their incompatibility. Nothing will resolve their hatred and/or complete lack of love for each other. Thus, nothing will make their marriage better. So, forget easy.

Every married person must pay attention to their marriage. First class marriages happen for good reasons. As highlighted later, a married person needs to be caring and attentive. A married person needs to observe and listen carefully. Patience and self-control are essential to an easy marriage. These concepts have examples throughout this book.

The six sections of <u>Easy Marriage</u> cover a variety of topics in addition to recommendations which bring pleasure and lightness into marriage. The *Foundation* section includes chapters on compatibility factors and long-lasting marriages.

The *Romantic Parts of Marriage* section has chapters on affection, romance, fun and marital friendship. The seven chapters of this section address the aspects of marriage which involve the pleasures of marriage.

The *Relationship Harmony* section is devoted to the interpersonal aspects of a marriage which either sink or swim a marriage. These chapters address topics such as: respect, humor anger, and appreciation. Some straightforward concepts and recommendations are concisely noted for handling everyday issues and problems.

The *Everyday Details* section includes another eleven chapters which address a potpourri of living-together aspects of marriage. The chapters include chores, house clutter, in-laws, mealtimes and other topics.

Easy Sex is the fifth section of <u>Easy Marriage</u>. There are twelve chapters with information and ideas for maintaining a vibrant and easy sexual relationship. Keep in mind that age, kids and length of marriage are not valid excuses for a dull or nonexistent sex life.

The *Organizing Your Marriage & Lifestyle* section includes chapters on lifestyle, vacations, evenings, weekends etc.

As you read along, keep in mind that the opposite of easy is difficult, stressful, chaotic and demanding. In other words, a toxic marriage of labor and drudgery.

Part I:
The Foundation

CHAPTER 1

Basic Parts of Marriage

—⚏—

I used to think that the worst thing in life was to
end up alone. It's not. The worst thing in life is
to end up with people who make you feel alone.
ROBIN WILLIAMS

THERE ARE FIVE BASIC PARTS to a marriage: lovers, friends, companions, partners, and parents. That's it. Not complicated. All marital issues and problems fall into one or more of these categories.

Each part brings potential pleasure and fulfillment into a marriage. Conversely, chronic problems in any part cause aggravation, conflict, disillusionment, and insidious wear and tear on a marriage. None of these parts should be neglected or mistreated. The importance of these parts should never be underestimated or dismissed.

When living together day after day, month after month and year after year, you and your spouse will be at your best and your worst, and everything in between. *An easy marriage is not only defined by a lack of problems, but also how a couple avoids and resolves problems.*

Because there will be conflicts and unhappiness at times in each of the parts, it is essential to make sure that there is a balance of pleasure in each of the parts.

Again, no part should be minimized, neglected or abused.

Being *lovers* involves: dating, romance, romantic affection, sex, flirting, seduction, romantic intimacy and physical attraction.

Being *friends* involves: communication, conversation, openness, trust, fun, pleasure and intimacy.

Being *companions* involves: spending time together, traveling, vacationing, and the simple pleasures that come from passing time together.

Being *partners* involves: chores, finances, household responsibilities, living together, shopping and joint decision-making on many matters. Think of it as the business side to the marriage.

Being *parents* involves: supervising, educating, loving, protecting, disciplining and nurturing your children. It should involve having fun with and enjoying your children throughout your life and their lives.

CHAPTER 2

Marriage Misconceptions

—⟋⟍—

Happiness is not a goal; it is a by-product.
ZEN BELIEF

EVERYONE HAS BELIEFS AND OPINIONS about marriage. In my career as a psychologist, sex therapist and marriage therapist, I have repeatedly encountered a variety of beliefs about marriage which interfere with marital happiness. Here are some key misconceptions about marriage:

Family is everything.
Sure, if it's a loving and healthy family. But what about families with relatives who steal from each other? Parents who abuse children? Domestic violence? Drunken rages? Parents who abandon their children? Family is *far* from everything for many unfortunate people.

Don't force this idea on yourself or others. Not everyone has a loving and supportive family.

All marital problems are 50 percent the fault of each spouse.
No. This is no more than a trendy cliché. Some marital problems are 100 percent the fault of one person.

Romantic love is unconditional.
This is a complete fabrication. Love is *always* conditional. In other words, love can be easily destroyed from abuse and neglect.

Spouses should not complacently think they can do whatever they want and yet still be loved. Romantic love can be ruined, wrecked and shattered. It is not unconditional.

In marriage, there are three sides to every issue: his, hers and the truth.
No. This is another trivial cliché. To begin with, the truth is the truth. Anyone can be prone to consciously or unconsciously lie, distort and exaggerate.

Some people will stop at nothing to get their way, including how they perceive, remember, and handle the details of some situations.

Only women need affection and romance.
This is ridiculously false. The fact is that *some men divorce their wives because of a lack of affection and romance, even when the sexual relationship is fine.*

Wanting and needing are different. Some men have to have affection and romantic intimacy in their marriage. They will not stay married without it.

Communication is the key to everything.
Not at all. The best communicators in the world can't resolve all marital problems.

However, some marital problems can *only* be resolved with good communication.

A very common problem is that some people think they are good communicators—but they are not. *Simply having a lot to say doesn't make you a good communicator.* Furthermore, being a good listener is as important as being able to express yourself.

Happy couples don't argue.
A naive thought. An exchange of opposite opinions occurs in all marriages. All couples disagree on some things. And of course, the disagreements may become passionate. What differentiates good from bad marriages is how people handle their conflicts and disagreements.

Sex always goes downhill once you're married.
In some marriages, the sex actually goes downhill on the honeymoon!

For some couples, sex gets better as the years go by. Maybe the sex is not as frequent, but sex gets markedly better and more enjoyable for *some* couples.

You should not expect sex to get worse because you are married. Also, less frequent does not automatically equate to a problem.

Once you have kids, the romance is over.
Adulthood is a sequence of stages—or chapters—of different lengths and life experiences. In problematic marriages, some spouses look for any reason—including pregnancy and having children—to terminate the romance and sex in the marriage. For some devious people, this was their plan from the beginning.

Conversely, some couples never tolerate a lack of marital romance just because of pregnancy, babies, children or adolescents at home.

Loving, healthy couples show their love for each other, with or without children! These are the people who make sure their romance doesn't fizzle out.

Marriage is the key to happiness.
Sorry. Not true. As indicated earlier, *there is no one guaranteed pathway to happiness in life.* Having children is not the pathway to happiness for everybody. Living in a city is not for everybody. Owning a house isn't the key for everyone. Living on a serene lake is not for everybody. And being married is not the key to happiness for everybody.

CHAPTER 3

Compatibility Versus Similarity

—⁓—

We were happily married for eight months.
Unfortunately, we were married
for four and a half years.
NICK FALDO

Some people say they got divorced because
they were like oil and water.
The truth is that they got divorced because
they were like two peas in a pod.
BRUCE FRIEDIN

Women marry men hoping they will change.
Men marry women hoping they will not.
Each is inevitably disappointed.
ALBERT EINSTEIN

*You don't really know a person
until you divorce them.*

?

FOR AN EASY MARRIAGE, SPOUSES don't have to be similar; they have to be compatible.

Similarity refers to having resemblance. It means being of the same nature.

Compatibility refers to *existing together in harmony.*

A harmonious marriage is much more important than whether you both love pizza, drive fast cars, or play golf.

Compatibility is what determines a good marriage, not whether you both have the same career or you are both of the same ethnic background.

There has always been an unfortunate myth that being of the same religion, or having the same hobbies, or coming from the same neighborhood are the factors which cause two people to be harmonious.

Although two people can have enormous romantic attraction for each other, it doesn't mean they can live harmoniously together.

Of course, similarity can be an important factor in marriage. But above all, harmony is what you need to have. Similarity doesn't automatically cause harmony.

Good marriages inherently have compatibility. Much of it is there from the start. Yet, some compatibility develops over time.

To have compatibility, there often has to be compromise. Compromise on any issue means neither one gets what he or she wanted.

If you have trouble with compromise, finding a happy medium, making concessions and meeting your partner halfway at times, marriage is probably not for you.

CHAPTER 4

To Marry or Not To Marry

—ᴍᴍ—

They keep saying the right person will come along.
I think mine got hit by a truck.

?

THE ASTRONOMICAL DIVORCE RATE INDICATES that as a society, we're not successful at marriage. Furthermore, our society has not been successful at rectifying this situation.

We know how to *get* married. We just don't *stay* married. And we don't know how to stay married *enjoyably*.

We know how to pick out wedding dresses and invitations and make seating arrangements. But we just don't know how to *have* a good marriage.

Perhaps brides and grooms should be picking out a therapist before they get married for screening—before they spend huge amounts of time and money picking out reception flowers and wedding bands.

Have you watched any reality shows with raging brides-to-be? Do you think these demanding women become sweet and gentle wives down the road? I don't think so.

There's no doubt that some marriages don't last because of incompatibility. Partly, they weren't a good match to begin with. For some couples, there's also no doubt that the handwriting was on the wall from the beginning. They either knew it would happen, or they ignored the signs that their relationship would end up in divorce.

However, some people do marry the *right* person, but they don't know how to maintain a happy, healthy marriage. Basically, they screw it up till there's nothing enjoyable left. Very sad.

The questions are obvious: How do people get to the point of marital misery? Where'd they go wrong? Why were they attracted to the wrong person? Were they never in love in the first place? Did they fall in love with someone else? Did their spouse change after marriage? Did they fall out of love?

How does a couple go from a 200 person wedding extravaganza to a vicious divorce a year later? How does a young couple go from a luscious Caribbean honeymoon to divorce court? Why are we so inept at marriage?

My advice is that when you think you are ready for engagement or marriage with someone, ask yourself the following questions. Then carefully assess your answers. These are not trivial questions. They have everything to do with future marital happiness or marital misery.

I'm not suggesting that you create a rigid checklist of requirements before marriage, but you should know what to look for regarding your future contentment, harmony and happiness in your marriage.

- Do I truly respect this fiancée?
- Do I love this person for who they are and not for who I want them to be down the road?
- Do I admire this man?
- Am I proud of my fiancée?
- Do I know how to show respect to a woman/man?
- Does s/he show respect to others?
- Are either of you verbally or physically abusive?
- Am I *very* satisfied with the quality of our communication?
- Are you a good listener?
- Is s/he a good listener?
- Do we compromise well?
- Do I know how to compromise?
  (If you don't believe in compromise, don't get married. Save yourselves the trouble.)
- Why do I want to spend the rest of my life with this person?
- Is s/he a nurturing person?

- Is s/he a happy person?
- Does s/he have a good outlook on life?
- Do we have a very good friendship?

- Can I live with this person and what they're like when they're very angry?
- Do either of us have serious temper problems?
- Do we handle conflict well?
- Do we have compatible parenting values?
- Do we accept and tolerate each other's hobbies?
- Do we have similar preferences regarding household cleanliness and clutter?
- Do we have compatible spending habits?
- Do we have compatible ideas and desires regarding management of finances?
- Do we have compatible feelings toward each other's families?
- Do we have compatible values regarding religion, even if we are of the same religion?
- Do we truly enjoy sex with each other?
- Can I live with this person's sexual desires and preferences?
- Am I okay with his/her drinking habits?
- Am I *positive* that neither one of us has a drinking or substance abuse problem?
- Do we have compatible values about work and income?
- Am I happy with how s/he takes care of his or her body and appearance?
- Are we compatible regarding grooming and hygiene?
- Do we both have pride in ourselves?

* Am I definitely accepting of his/her health problems?
* Am I accepting of his/her physical attributes?

* Do I have fun with this person?
* Do we have fun together?
* Will his/her family be a major problem for me or for us?
* Do I really trust this person?
* Did s/he lie about prior marriages when we met?
* How often do I catch him/her in a lie?
* What are the lies a about?
* Did s/he lie about prior credit card debt?
* Is s/he honest when s/he's angry?
* Does s/he pretend s/he's not angry?
* Is there a history of multiple infidelities in previous relationships and marriages?
* I know or suspect s/he's had sexual encounters with same sex partners, but s/he says s/he's not gay. Should I believe him/her?
* Do we have good conversation on a regular basis?

Now...what are your responses to these questions? Is anything problematic jumping out at you? Are the questions and your answers making you nervous or uncomfortable?

If you have serious concerns, you and your partner need to have serious talks. You may also want to consult with a professional.

CHAPTER 5

Predicting Your Marriage Will Last

—⟋⟋⟋—

True love stories never have endings.
RICHARD BACH

How many husbands have I had?
You mean apart from my own?
ZSA ZSA GABOR

GETTING MARRIED IS VERY EASY. As you know, anyone can do it. You could be a serial killer on death row or look like Quasimodo— anybody can find someone, somewhere, somehow to marry them.

Staying married is a challenge. And staying *happily and satisfyingly* married is *extremely* difficult—if you don't know how. And most people don't know how. Which is why marriage feels like work to most people.

It's fair to say that at the time of a wedding, most people are not contemplating such crises as future infidelity or divorce. Newly married people are more or less basking in the good spirits and blissfulness of their marriage.

But then the weeks and months go by. Without the main ingredients of good romance and good compatibility, people eventually don't want to stay married. They may *have* to stay married, but they don't *want* to be married.

Romantic attraction is what gets most relationships started. Incompatibility is what often kills off a relationship.

The problem for many couples is that one or both spouses realize they're incompatible after it's too late (i.e., they're already married and have children). On a side note, this is why it can be a worthwhile experience to live together before you marry. But the same rule applies: with or without the marriage part, you have to know how to live well together.

My firm advice is that you should not ignore major incompatibilities before you get married. Don't pretend that problems don't exist.

For example, don't think that sex will automatically get better after you marry. Don't fool yourself that alcoholism will automatically get better. Don't bet that your husband is going to watch less TV. Don't bet that your fiancée is going to finally become an honest person later in the marriage.

The main problems which kill a marriage: lack of romance; lack of love; the inability to resolve conflicts; poor compatibility; poor communication; chronic anger: and loss of romantic attraction.

Don't get married just so that you can say you are married.

Have you really contemplated what it would be like to be with this person one, five, or ten years from now? Are you positive you know this person?

I sometimes use an expression that some marriages just "run out of gas." This is where both spouses fell out of love with each other. They don't hate each other. Love doesn't just automatically go on forever. Even when some people treat each other very well, their relationship can become joyless and lifeless.

What's important is whether you know how to maintain a rewarding relationship. Some people are not necessarily committing major transgressions, but they're sucking the soul out of the marriage by not trying to have a close relationship as friends and lovers. The end result: their attitude reaches the lowest point of preferring to be single rather than staying married.

Part II: The Romantic Parts of Marriage

CHAPTER 6

Affection

—ɯɯ—

Do you know what it means to come home at night
to a woman who'll give you a little love,
a little affection, a little tenderness?
It means you're in the wrong house.
HENNY YOUNGMAN

Do anything rather than marry without affection.
JANE AUSTEN

She gave me a smile I could feel in my hip pocket.
RAYMOND CHANDLER

IS A MARRIAGE WITHOUT AFFECTION worth having? Some people
don't think so. Affection refers to the actual expression—both verbal and physical—of fond feelings to another person. Romantic
affection is the type of affection that you *wouldn't* show to relatives or friends.

Romantic affection refers to the kissing, holding, touching, caressing, fondling that occurs in a romantic relationship. Romantic affection also refers to when a person expresses tender, warm, loving feelings. In other words, you wouldn't kiss grandma this way.

For some people, a marriage without affection is worse than living alone. When you're in a marriage with minimal or no affection, you feel starved, deprived, frustrated, and highly conflicted about the marriage. It is not unusual to feel stripped of your self-worth when you don't have affection from your spouse.

A lack of affection can be both a symptom and a cause of serious marital problems. Whatever is wrong in the marriage, address and fix it as soon as possible. Don't ignore it. Ideally, you always want the road clear for affection. Get rid of the obstacles and detours.

Affection is one of the most enjoyable aspects of marriage. You can give and receive it every day. A touch, a hug, a caress, a smile, a look, a word, a few words. Sometimes, only a tiny amount of effort is involved.

Because it is natural to be affectionate when dating a person you're attracted to, an unaffectionate person is sending a signal of disinterest. Don't think that the unaffectionate boy/girlfriend is going to be an affectionate spouse.

Children who grow up without adequate love, nurturance, protection and affection will likely grow up with psychological conflicts and problems. This is why a child can be raised by a loving grand-mother and be perfectly healthy and happy, and yet a child raised by two unloving parents may suffer terribly as an adult.

Even if you grew up in a home in which your parents showed little affection to each other, to you and/or to your siblings, it is vital *not* to continue this pattern into your marriage and family. Get whatever help you need in order to learn to enjoy giving and receiving affection.

Affection has nourishing and sustaining qualities. Many marriages fall apart not because of a lack of sex but because of a lack of affection! Couples may be more likely to stay together with affection but no sex compared to couples who have sex and no romantic affection.

CHAPTER 7

Friendship &
Companionship

—⟋⟍⟋—

Ultimately, the bond of all companionship,
whether in marriage or in
friendship, is conversation.
OSCAR WILDE

It is not a lack of love, but a lack of friendship
that makes unhappy marriages.
F. NIETZSCHE

Friends are God's way of apologizing
to us for our families.
?

I know nothing in the world that
has as much power as a word.
EMILY DICKINSON

HERE'S A BASIC CONCEPT: YOU can't have a good marriage without friendship.

A husband and wife don't have to be best friends in order to have a good marriage, but they must be close friends. Best friends are often of the same gender, and sometimes their friendship began early in life.

Close friends trust each other. Close friends confide in each other. They treat each other with respect. They're happy for each other's successes and happiness. They have fun together. But above everything, they enjoy opening up to each other and they enjoy listening to each other. *Their bond is conversation!*

You can't expect to have a long-term happy marriage without friendship. The friendship in a marriage often has to be the top priority. Your work, your chores, and your children shouldn't always be the top priority in life—if you want to be happy in your marriage.

Have you noticed that you open up to your really close friends more than you talk to your spouse? Have you noticed that you don't verbally abuse your close friends the way you verbally abuse your spouse?

If you're answering "yes" to these questions, you need to address this serious problem. If this goes unchecked, it could potentially and eventually cause the end of your marriage.

If you don't communicate well or enjoy each other's company, friendship will not thrive and it makes a marriage very difficult. If the friendship doesn't thrive, the marriage won't survive.

It's obvious to many people that part of a good marriage is when you have similar interests. But you don't need to have the same hobbies to have a close friendship.

CHAPTER 8

Dating Your Spouse

—ᜃ—

We'll always have Paris.
Casablanca

Remember you were a girlfriend
before you were a mother.
My Big Fat Greek Wedding 2

In the overall course of a marriage, Saturday night should not feel like a Tuesday night. Weekends shouldn't feel like weekdays.

It's healthy and refreshing to have some variation in your routines and daily expectancies. And it's healthy to be able to look forward to pleasurable experiences. Variety is the spice of life, and spices are the variety of life.

Having enjoyable time with your spouse can be romantic and even sexy. And it can even be foreplay for sex.

As a couple, getting away from the kids and the house can be refreshing. And don't think you have to spend any or even a lot of money.

Although many couples try to have a regular date night, it can be a challenge to have the same date night every week. You don't need to lock into a specific date night.

Some couples claim they can't find or don't have a babysitter. For other couples, they just don't trust anyone to watch their kids. Suffice it to say that if you and your spouse don't somehow figure out how to have enjoyable time together on some type of regular basis, the likelihood is that your marriage will suffer.

I don't believe it's a good idea for couples to only see each other in sweatsuits and old jeans all the time. If you remember earlier in your life when you first met each other and you were attracted to and wanted to see other again, you wanted to look good for each other. You wanted him/her to be attracted to you. This shouldn't end after you get married. Why would you even want this to end?

Marriage can be so much more effortless, painless, and easygoing when you take the time to enjoy each other's company.

CHAPTER 9

Intimacy

—ᴍ—

His voice was as intimate as the rustle of sheets.
Dᴏʀᴏᴛʜʏ Pᴀʀᴋᴇʀ

*For a woman, there is nothing more erotic
than being understood.*
Mᴏʟʟʏ Hᴀꜱᴋᴇʟʟ

*When my soul was in the lost-and-found,
you came along to claim it.
I didn't know what was wrong with me
till your kiss helped me to name it.
Now I'm no longer doubtful of what I'm living for.
Because if I make you happy, I don't need anything
more. Because you make me feel,
you make me feel like a natural woman.*
Cᴀʀᴏʟᴇ Kɪɴɢ

WITHOUT INTIMACY, YOU CANNOT POSSIBLY have a good marriage. Intimacy requires closeness, comfort and safety. There has to be trust at the highest levels. You have to be able to open up and be good listeners to each other.

A non-intimate marriage is a very difficult marriage. Stifling yourself because you have a non-interested spouse is disheartening and draining. And living with a partner who prevents and avoids intimacy is exasperating and painful.

For the record, there is a difference between thoughts (cognitive) and feelings (emotional). Thoughts refer to ideas, beliefs, opinions, and judgments. Feelings refer to sadness, shame, guilt, anger embarrassment, happiness etc.

Intimate closeness comes from expressing/sharing both thoughts and feelings. Intimacy makes a marriage feel very comfortable. Very right.

There are two kinds of generosity: generosity with money and gifts. And generosity of the heart—the most meaningful of the two.

Generosity of the heart involves an unselfish type of kindness. It is a type of warmhearted *givingness.* Giving your time and the giving of your attention to your spouse helps create and maintain a gratifying and pleasing relationship.

How giving are you?

CHAPTER 10

Romance

Romance is everything.
<small>GERTRUDE STEIN</small>

Men always want to be a woman's first love.
Women like to be a man's last romance.
<small>OSCAR WILDE</small>

When I saw you, I was afraid to meet you...
When I met you, I was afraid to kiss you...
When I kissed you, I was afraid to love you...
Now that I love you, I'm afraid to lose you.
?

A MARRIAGE BETWEEN A MAN and a woman is truly a mixed marriage.

If you're the husband, you need to remember that you married a woman. She looks, acts, thinks and feels like a woman. Do not treat her as if she's man. And don't expect her to think like a man. If you treat her like a man, maybe you should have married a man. Speak to her and treat her with respect at all times.

You need to understand what it means to be a good man and a good husband. If you want a high quality and easy marriage, treat your wife with love, affection and respect.

If you're the wife, you have to remember that you married a man. Chances are, he looks, acts, feels and thinks like most men. Don't expect him to have feminine traits. Don't emasculate him.

When couples respect and enjoy their similarities and differences and they know how to compromise and show good will to each to each other, a marriage is likely to be enjoyable. There is a perfectly wide range of lifestyles that husbands and wives can have which suit their personalities and values.

Some men and women have a tendency to experience romance as work rather than play. Through good communication, and some attention and some experimenting, romance can eventually be experienced as mutually enjoyable—thus making a marriage much easier and so much nicer.

If romantic attention feels like hard work, I suggest that you need to examine yourself. Don't be negligent in your marriage. Figure out what's wrong. Talk about it. You didn't get married to suffer.

But what is romance? Why is this so hard for some people? Why does it die out in some marriages?

Romance involves a combination of affection, passion and loving feelings. Romance can be expressed in many pleasurable ways. Devotion and affectionate kindness ideally feels good and feels right.

Remember, if you psychologically beat up a marriage enough, you'll eventually kill the romance and love.

A marriage is not indestructible. Just like a seemingly indestructible marble statue, if you ding the base once a day with a hammer, eventually it will topple over.

It's not as if couples need to be constantly sweet to each other. But there should be a blend of warmth, tenderness, kindness, sentiment and coziness in a marriage.

CHAPTER 11

Love

—⟋⟍—

*The way to love anything is to realize it
might be lost.*
G. CHESTERTON

*The story of love is not important;
what is important is that one is capable of love.
It is perhaps the only glimpse we are permitted
of eternity.*
HELEN HAYES

*Do you love me because I'm beautiful,
or am I beautiful because you love me?*
OSCAR HAMMERSTEIN II

*Better to have loved and lost, my ass.
Anyone parroting that little
platitude has obviously never
lost anyone of consequence.*
NENIA CAMPBELL

A bell is no bell 'til you ring it,
A song is no song 'til you sing it,
And love in your heart wasn't put there to stay.
Love isn't love 'til you give it away.
OSCAR HAMMERSTEIN

If grass can grow through cement,
love can find you at every time in your life.
CHER

You can give without loving,
but you can never love without giving.

?

SCIENTISTS AND POETS HAVE TRIED to define and quantify romantic love for centuries, yet there is no clear cut formula or definition.

Is it even possible for a married couple to have an easy marriage if they're not in love with each other? Actually, it is possible, depending on their ability to have a peaceful co-existence.

There are many people who claim to love each other yet treat each other terribly. Which leads to the question why do people hurt the ones they love? The answers to this question are extraordinarily complex and way beyond the scope of this book.

A few things about love can be highlighted. First of all, romantic love doesn't begin with a wedding. Love begins with an attraction, desires to be close and caring, and the desire to be romantically intimate on every level.

Many healthy feelings, thoughts and actions should emanate from romantic love: respect, affection, kindness, passion, attachment, devotion and lust.

Sadly, however, there are many broken people in this world. Broken in the sense of how they were raised and what occurred in their developmental years (about the first twenty years of life). Love is something painfully complicated for them. Love is difficult for them to show. It can even be scary, if not petrifying, for them to feel and surrender to romantic love.

Try to imagine that love for a person can exist on a 'scale' from none to passionate. Ideally, marital love between two people is about equal, yet not down at the *none* level.

There will always be marital problems if the love between two spouses is not roughly equal. Problems will likely arise because of a fundamental corollary: The one who loves significantly less controls the marriage. The one who loves disproportionally more will often have to make concessions and sacrifices in order to please the one who loves less. This is never good for a marriage.

Even in a marriage with a seriously disproportionate amount of love, it is sometimes possible to fix the problems which are causing the disparity. Then, perhaps, the love can be mutually comparable.

Again, romantic love is not unconditional. Quite the opposite. Love is very conditional. Although love can grow, it can also be destroyed. Don't take risks by hurting your spouse.

Romantic love doesn't automatically survive forever. Love can be eroded and ruined, little by little, in a bad marriage. Love can be destroyed to a point in which nothing will ever bring it back no matter how hard anyone tries.

What really are the most important questions in life? I believe that the two most profoundly important questions in life are: What is worth living for, and what is worth dying for? I think the consummate answer to these questions is the same single word: love. Romantic love. Love of your children. Love of your friends and relatives.

CHAPTER 12

Fun

*I was a quiet, boring child. Whenever we played doctor,
the other kids made me the anesthesiologist.*
RITA RUDNER

He had to die to prove he was alive.
?

Make her laugh and you will have her heart.
?

I don't do bored.
?

Laughter is the valve on the pressure cooker of life.
WAVY GRAVY

All you need in the world is love and laughter.
AUGUST WILSON

WE ALL UNDERSTAND THAT SOME unhappily married people stay married because of financial or children-related reasons. But do you *want* a dull, boring marriage?

A lifeless, uninspiring, insipid marriage is a difficult and painful marriage.

Fun can be defined as lighthearted pleasure, amusement, entertainment, or recreation. Pleasure and lightheartedness have the ability to make living together an easy journey through life.

With or without children, married people should have fun at times. You should enjoy your marriage. You didn't get married in order to live your life in a stale, lackluster marriage.

A happy marriage includes: fun with their friends, fun with other couples, fun with hobbies and fun with each other.

When I've asked some married people if they have fun, they've looked at me as if I had two heads. They hadn't thought about having fun since they were dating.

Remember: fun is not just for children. You didn't get married to suffer or stay bored.

Part III:
Relationship Harmony

*I must be a mermaid.
I have no fear of depth and a
great fear of shallow living.*
ANAIS NIN

Shut your eyes and see.
JAMES JOYCE

SO, DO YOU THINK YOU'RE easy to live with? Really? You checked yourself before you answered? Okay, here are some more self-evaluation questions: Do you help out with taking care of your home even though you work full-time? If you don't work outside the home, do you show respect and express appreciation for your spouse who does? Do you leave messes for your spouse to clean up?

Do you flagrantly check social media during meals with your spouse at home or in restaurants? Do you text during meals? Do you check or read email during meals? Do you check sports scores or email during meals? Do you make or answer phone calls during meals? Do you really think that's not obnoxious, or do you just don't care if you're obnoxious?

How nasty and hurtful are you when you're angry? Is the family scared of you? Do you care if they're scared of you? Do you stay angry for days? Do you punish your spouse with silence for days?

How much do you drink? Do you really think smoking marijuana on a daily basis is harmless? It's not. Do you really think you're the same whether you're stoned or not? You're not.

Do you think you're patient with your spouse? You do take the time to sit, make eye contact and listen?

You've proven you're an honest person? Are you friends with your spouse? Close friends? Best friends?

Do you care if your spouse is sexually attracted to you, or do you just want sex?

How demanding are you? How controlling are you? How self-centered are you? Are you arrogant or pompous to your spouse? Do you pout or go into rages when you don't get your way?

Do you share the TV remote? Are you willing to spend some time alone with your spouse after work on some days?

Do you try to enjoy your spouse? Do you enjoy your kids?

Are you fortunate to have your spouse? Is your spouse fortunate to have you? Are you a great catch?

Do you hope your child grows up and marries someone who has your qualities? Someone just like you? Do you hope your child has a marriage just like yours?

The point is that these questions should provoke self-examination and examination of what you want your marriage to be.

CHAPTER 13

Communication

—〰—

Love without conversation is impossible.
MORTIMER ADLER

Most people do not listen with
the intent to understand.
They listen with the intent to reply.
?

Speak in such a way that others love
to listen to you. Listen in such a way
that others love to speak to you.
?

Don't say maybe when you want to say no.
PAULO COELHO

*My wife talks to me in code.
Instead of making requests to me, she asks
questions. If I forget and leave my underwear
on the floor, she says, "Are these yours?"*
JEFF ALLEN

COMMUNICATION PROBLEMS ARE WHAT OFTEN compel couples into marital therapy. Such problems range from rarely speaking to each other to raging arguments. Always talking to never listening to each other. Picking the worst places or the worst times to have a discussion.

An easy marriage requires that you have interesting conversations at least some of the time. It doesn't matter what other couples find interesting; it has to be interesting to you. Conversation has to create satisfaction.

The Good Listener
Being a good listener is as important as being able to express yourself. Being a good listener means *showing* respect when your spouse is talking.

A good listener shows s/he's listening by: body language, eye contact and facial expressions. It really does matter to *show* that you're listening. Don't just claim you are listening while you're looking at your phone. Your reactions, comments and questions show that you are listening attentively.

Some Guidelines

Don't have important conversations with the TV on. Don't look at your phone or a computer screen. Or the newspaper. Or while doing chores. Or while driving a vehicle 50mph. Or if one or both of you is intoxicated.

In terms of expressing yourself, have you been told you have any annoying habits? Do you talk down to your spouse? Do you give advice even when you're not asked for any? Are you often requested to lower your voice and not yell? Do you mumble? Do you exaggerate?

Do you make vague requests and expect your spouse to know *exactly* what you meant? Do you expect your spouse to read your mind regarding what you meant? Do you get angry when s/he doesn't read your mind?

Communication is important to all parts of a marriage. When having any kind of important discussion, discipline yourself as follows: don't raise your voice when frustrated; don't exaggerate; take your time; don't be disrespectful; and be patient. Know when to be very specific.

Overall, try to be as responsive as possible to complaints. Pay attention to what bothers your spouse when and how you're conversing.

If a topic is much more important to your spouse than it is to you, you still should be respectful and patient when listening.

<u>Conversation Starter</u>
The statement "We need to talk" always seems to have a grim tone to it. Accordingly, the spouse will immediately feel defensive.

Try these options: "When you have a few minutes, I'd like to talk about…" "Let me know when the show is over so we can discuss…" "I need five minutes to talk to you about…" Avoid having an ominous tone.

Talking about "your day" is quite the turn-off for some people. The *"How was your day?"* question, even to children, is often a tedious question to answer. For some people, talking about their day will get them needlessly upset all over again.

In general: No whining. Don't talk over each other. Don't interrupt. Don't repeat yourself. Make some eye contact when you speak and listen.

Some people have no difficulty with conversation at work or with friends. If that's the case but you and your spouse converse very little, you both should take steps to resolve this. Basically, if you're talking very little to each other, it's likely time for some professional help.

Some people have struggled a lifetime with speaking and assertion. Some people shrug it off as shyness. Sometimes it's a much more significant concern.

Social anxiety refers to a fear of sounding dumb and being embarrassed. It may involve a fear of offending others. It involves irrational self-consciousness. The good news is that it is a collection of problems that can be alleviated with professional help.

Desires, Wishes & Needs
There is this colloquial expression that many people use that refers to their *needs*. "My needs are…" "He's not meeting my needs." This word (and its implication of necessity) is way over-used and often inappropriately used.

If you're going to use the word *needs*, it means that if you don't get them met, there will be major conflict, if not divorce. If that's the case, then you are using the word correctly.

Otherwise, frame your requests with wording involving wants, wishes and desires. This may sound as if I'm splitting semantic hairs, but saying you *want* something is not the same as saying you *must* have something.

Making Promises
If your spouse requests a favor or a chore—and you agree to it—you just signed a contract! You signed on the dotted line.

What many people don't understand is that if your spouse follows up with you because you haven't completed the task (as you *promised*)—it's not nagging! In other words, don't break your own promises. If you signed the contract, just follow through. Otherwise, don't sign in the first place.

To put it another way, don't make promises/sign contracts just to dismiss your spouse. Expect to be held accountable when you make a promise.

Starting a Conversation With a Preface

A book's preface is often the last part of a book that's written. Yet it exists at the beginning of a book. Similarly, it often helps to begin an important conversation with a preface of your topics and the potential difficulties.

The following examples illustrate helpful prefaces:

"I want to talk with you about…but I'm not attacking you."

"I want to tell you something, but I really hope you don't get upset or think I'm criticizing you."

"I have to ask you something, but I hope you don't get defensive."

"I think we should discuss…but we both need to stay calm."

"We need to discuss…but give me a chance to finish what I want to say first before we discuss it."

The One-Way Conversation

A *one way conversation* is actually a misnomer. I frame it like this because there are many times when it is more helpful for one spouse to say what they want to say while the other spouse just listens carefully—and doesn't respond…they just listen.

When one spouse feels attacked, they are likely to get defensive. They are likely to attack back. They may even blame the spouse for their behavior. The two-way conversation can then become a painful waste of time.

When one spouse is asked to just sit back, listen and not respond or interrupt, they often listen carefully.

The preface would go like this:

"I want to tell you something, and I don't want to discuss it. I just want you to listen to what I have to say."

"I want to tell you something, and I really don't want to hear your explanation. I just want you to listen and try to understand why I'm so angry/upset etc."

Then, when you say what you want, just walk away. Let them think about what you said, and hopefully they'll appreciate the issues in what you said.

Re-visiting an Issue or Problem

It's impossible to always have a perfect response to a sudden and unexpected criticism or complaint. It's also impossible to always think of all the things you'd like to say during a conversation.

Instead of criticizing yourself or harboring resentment, just bring up the topic at a later hour, or the next day or even the next week. It would go like this:

"Do you remember when we were talking about…?" I also want to add…"

"I have to tell you that I'm still upset/angry with what you said to me yesterday."

"I want you to know that I'm still upset with that argument we had over the weekend. There are still loose ends for me."

Knowing that you can almost always re-visit an important topic, it makes it easier to handle unexpected situations in which you didn't say everything you wanted.

CHAPTER 14

Appreciation

—〰—

*Let us be grateful to the people who make us
happy. They are the charming gardeners who make
our souls blossom.*

MARCEL PROUST

*I've learned that people will forget what you said.
People will forget what you did.
But people will never forget how
you made them feel.*

MAYA ANGELOU

*Appreciate what you have before it turns into
what you had.*

?

*Today is a gift.
That's why it's called the present.*

?

Silent gratitude isn't much use to anyone.
G.B. STERN

*Feeling gratitude and not expressing it is like
wrapping a present and not giving it.*
WILLIAM WARD

APPRECIATION IS HIGHLY UNDERVALUED AND under-expressed in most marriages. It is sadly common for spouses to expect that their spouse will work, do chores, do projects…just because.

Do not underestimate the value of expressing appreciation to your spouse. It's important to feel valued. To feel worth. No wants to be trivialized. No one wants their contributions to a marriage, family and home to be trivialized.

Although spouses may have their different chores and responsibilities, it's very supportive to express appreciation for each other's efforts around the home. Don't go through life with blinders on. Take notice of your spouse's efforts.

Thank your spouse even for the little things. Even a quick hug can say thank you. Don't be cheap with thankyou's.

It's a good thing when you thank your spouse for doing household chores or preparing a nice meal. It's a good thing when you acknowledge your spouse for working overtime. It's a good thing to be appreciated for going out of your way to do a favor. It won't kill you to say thanks. And it doesn't cost anything. And it only takes a second.

No one wants to be taken for granted.

Respect

—ʍ—

I can't keep running into the same knives.
?

If you don't respect her, you don't deserve her.
?

I speak to everyone the same way whether he is the garbage man or the president of the university.
ALBERT EINSTEIN

Girls want attention.
Women want respect.
?

THERE PROBABLY HASN'T BEEN A marriage ceremony anywhere in the world without a reference to the importance of respect. And yet it's a vow that many people violate on a regular basis from day one of their marriage.

You cannot have a good marriage without mutual respect. It's impossible. Respect is defined as feelings of admiration. It involves politeness, civility and deference. Being respectful involves being well-mannered, courteous and gracious.

The parts of respect include what you *feel* in addition to how you *show* it. Disrespect is detrimental if not ruinous to a marriage. If you *get away* with showing or expressing disrespect to your spouse, you will eventually feel disrespect. The more you feel disrespect, the more you will show it. And it just gets worse from there.

Feeling and showing respect are essential to all healthy relationships of any kind.

The chronic problem of feeling and showing disrespect should drive you into obtaining professional help. Underlying anger is not always what it may seem. Sometimes disrespect has its roots as far back as early childhood and your parents' marriage. Chronic disrespect will erode a marriage. It will make a marriage increasingly difficult.

Disrespect should not be tolerated, ignored or overlooked. At the least, disrespect requires an apology. If you have difficulty with apologies and you believe you don't need professional help, maybe you shouldn't be married.

Being angry is not an excuse for disrespect. You cannot force your spouse to feel respect, but you can refuse to be disrespected.

CHAPTER 16

Patience

—𝔪—

Have you ever noticed that anybody
driving slower than you is an idiot,
and anyone going faster than you is a maniac?
GEORGE CARLIN

The key to everything is patience.
You get the chicken by hatching the egg,
not by smashing it.
ARNOLD H. GLASGOW

Patience is also a form of action.
AUGUSTE RODIN

Patience is the companion of wisdom.
ST. AUGUSTINE

One moment of patience may ward off great disaster. One moment of impatience may ruin a whole life.
CHINESE PROVERB

MARRIED COUPLES HAVE A TENDENCY to *not* have the same level of patience with each other that they have for everyone else, including strangers. Most married people do not yell, curse or talk down to their bosses and clients at work, and most people do not yell or curse at people in stores.

Many people have good control over their anger and frustration everywhere except at home. They walk in the front door and just let loose with saying and doing anything they want when they're angry.

No one deserves more patience than your spouse and children. They don't deserve being screamed at or cursed at. They don't deserve being belittled or humiliated because you're in a rush, or you had a tough day, or you got stuck in traffic or you have a lot on your mind.

Loved ones deserve that you take the time to manage your frustrations with patience, respect and calmness. Most of the things that get us stressed are not life and death situations. Overall, you should take the time to think before you express frustration, and to treat loved ones with the respect and dignity they deserve.

Multi-tasking is a fairly new term referring to the praiseworthy ability of doing multiple things simultaneously. Somehow, our society and the business world have caused people to believe this is a special skill. Really?

Is it okay if your heart surgeon takes phone calls during your surgery? Would you want your children in a car with a driver who is driving 55mph and texting?

Let's be real: performing multiple tasks simultaneously means you're not giving your full attention to anything. It causes you to do almost nothing accurately. Multi-tasking causes internalized pressure and a false sense of accomplishment. Consider also that *time-saving* devices don't really save time. They allow you to do more things at once.

Multi-taskers unfortunately expect others to be multi-taskers also. This can get way out of hand at home.

Don't expect your family to read your mind, understand sarcastic questions or understand your vague requests. Instead of yelling at your spouse, "Why do you have to listen to the TV so loud?" just say, "Please lower the TV."

When you want your spouse to focus on what you have to say, take a few extra seconds to make sure you have your spouse's attention. Don't just start talking to them from another room.

The more things you do simultaneously, the more you are compressing your sense of time and feeling overwhelmed. You don't necessarily accomplish more, especially since you are not giving anything your full attention to any one thing.

<u>A Metaphor for Patience</u>
Most people have never contemplated the difference between cooking and baking. I'll explain.

With cooking, you can spontaneously cook a chicken with all kinds and combinations of spices and other ingredients—just making it all up as you go along—and it could quite possibly turn out delicious. Of course, it could be quite the opposite.

With baking (e.g., breads, cakes and pies), you have to methodically follow a recipe. If the recipe says two cups flour, you can't just add one cup. If the recipe calls for one half teaspoon of baking powder, you can't add one tablespoon. If the recipe says bake at 350 degrees for 40 minutes, you can't bake it for 500 degrees for 20 minutes because you're impatient. Violate the recipe and you will automatically create something inedible.

When you need to have an important conversation with your spouse—*bake* it and do it right the first time. Carefully and patiently take the time. Don't take a chance and *throw together* a conversation that could turn into a complete mess.

Take your time!

CHAPTER 17

Not Begging For Attention

—ɯ—

Paying attention is a form of generosity.
?

NO ONE SHOULD HAVE TO beg for attention in their marriage. In a good marriage, neither spouse gets or settles for crumbs of attention. In this context, paying attention doesn't just mean listening. It means having the desire to spend time together.

Paying attention to your spouse has different components. It involves being a good listener and a good communicator. It involves showing that you both want, or are willing, to spend time knowing: each other's thoughts, feelings, desires, what makes them happy and what makes them upset. It means showing consideration. Being thoughtful. Being kind, understanding and compassionate.

If you're satisfied with having a bad marriage, you can achieve that by ignoring, dismissing and/or trivializing your spouse. Conversely, if you're a person who requires a good marriage, then you have to give and receive attention to each other.

If giving attention to your spouse feels like work to you, you should dig deep and try to figure out why. Is it related to your parents' bad marriage? Do you have a selfish personality? Do you have chronic unresolved anger at your spouse? Is your spouse overly demanding? Suffocating? Are you chronically exhausted psychologically from work or life's demands? Do you feel like you need to be left alone all the time? In other words, this is not so easy to figure out.

Sometimes it's difficult giving attention to a spouse that is overly self-centered. For example, a spouse who frequently repeats issues or complaints. A spouse who wants or demands constant attention. A spouse who frequently just talks about one topic such as their work. If this is the case, this has to be openly addressed.

On a final note, when you are paying attention—do it right. Don't pretend you are listening. Don't be hostile. Don't be a martyr. You're not making a huge sacrifice.

Try to be generous with giving attention. Your spouse shouldn't have to chronically request or beg you for attention or spending some time together.

CHAPTER 18

Humor

—m—

Sexiness wears thin after a while and beauty fades.
But to be married to a man who makes you
laugh every day—
Ah, now that's a real treat.
JOANNE WOODWARD

Laughter and orgasm are great bedfellows.
JOHN CALLAHAN

There is purifying power in laughter.
EUGENE BERTIN

A big laugh is a really loud noise
from the soul saying,
"Ain't that the truth."
QUINCY JONES

If you are too busy to laugh,
you are too busy.
?

A good time to laugh is any time you can.
LINDA ELLERBEE

Have I told you lately that I love you?
Have I told you there's no one else above you?
Fill my heart with gladness, take
away all my sadness,
Ease my troubles, that's what you do.
The morning sun in all its glory,
Meets the day with hope and comfort too,
You fill my life with laughter and
somehow you make it better,
Ease my troubles, that's what you do.
VAN MORRISON

NOT EVERYBODY CAN TELL GOOD jokes or funny stories. Some people don't see humor in life, and they don't look for it. Some people don't watch comedies. Some people rarely chuckle, laugh or even smile.

Not that humor (i.e., playfulness, lightheartedness, silliness) is critical to marriage, but it definitely makes marriage and life enjoyable. And it certainly makes some life situations a lot easier.

Humor is a wonderful part of life and an ingredient for an easy marriage. There are so many aspects of life that are difficult or boring. Painful and frustrating. Stressful and grueling.

Humor spices up a marriage. It lightens up a marriage. It makes the journey through life much easier. It is unquestionably conducive to good mental and physical health.

Laughing together is also sexy. Some research studies indicate that humor draws single people together into courtship. In other words, it can be quite an aphrodisiac.

A husband and wife don't have to laugh at the same things in order to be compatible. It's just that laughter and humor are a great part of life and marriage. I strongly suggest that you try to look for and share humor in life as much as possible.

CHAPTER 19

Empathy

—⚏—

When you listen with empathy to another person,
you give that person psychological air.
STEPHEN R. COVEY

If there is any one secret of success,
it lies in the ability to get the
other person's point of view
and see things from his angle as well as your own.
HENRY FORD

When we honestly ask ourselves
which person in our lives
mean the most to us,
we often find that it is those who,
instead of giving advice,
solutions, or cures, have chosen
rather to share our pain
and touch our wounds with a
warm and tender hand.
The friend who can be silent with us in a
moment of despair or confusion,
who can stay with us in an hour
of grief and bereavement,
who can tolerate not knowing, not curing,
not healing and face with us the
reality of our powerlessness,
that is a friend who cares.
HENRI J.M. NOUWEN

I needed the shelter of someone's arms,
and there you were.
I needed someone to understand
my ups and downs,
and there you were.
With sweet love and devotion,
deeply touching my emotion.
I want to stop and thank you baby.
How sweet it is to be loved by you.
JAMES TAYLOR

HE SAYS: "BOY, DO I have a headache."
She says: "Take some Advil."

She says: "The traffic was terrible."
    He says: "You should have taken a different route."

Empathy is the compassionate ability to *understand* the feelings of others. Sympathy is the compassionate *feeling of sorrow* for someone's problems or misfortune. And compassion is the sympathetic concern for the suffering of others.

When a spouse talks about headaches, backaches, cramps, wrinkles, gray hairs, and traffic delays, it's not because they want advice. At the least, they likely want a little empathy. Serious problems may deserve sympathy too, but the everyday problems deserve empathy—not advice.

In the above example, he didn't need or want her to tell him to take medicine. He wasn't looking for unsolicited advice. And it's potentially aggravating, despite the wife's sincere attempt to be helpful.

A pretty good rule of thumb is to not give advice unless your spouse asks for it. So, the next time your spouse says they have stomach or back pain, you can offer something like, "Sorry to hear that. Can I get you anything?"

Empathy is being able to put yourself in the other person's position. Can you picture what they see? Can you imagine what they hear or what they feel? Do you understand why they're upset?

Empathy doesn't mean you have to agree with the other person's beliefs or opinions.

The person who is tearful but denies being upset is certainly hard to read. The person who is seemingly brooding and sullen but denies being angry is also hard to read. If you tend to fall in this category, you run the ongoing risk of having a spouse who cannot empathize with you.

Scientific studies show that women tend to be more empathic than men. Whereas women tend to be able to recognize a variety of emotions in others, men tend to be more adept at recognizing anger in others.

The bottom line is that we don't always know what to say to be supportive. We may even say something intended to be empathetic, and it backfires.

Many times over the decades, I've asked kids: "Does your father know you?" "Does your mother know you?" I've asked adults: "Do your kids know you?" "Did your parents know you?" "Does your wife/husband know you?"

The sadness is intensely palpable in the room when kids or adults say "No." With most individuals, this is the first time in their lives that they've contemplated this issue.

As you might guess, this causes a terribly empty feeling because it taps into a deep psychological abyss. In many families and marriages, however, this can be rectified.

Some people will never have an opportunity to open up to a child, parent, spouse or former spouse. For others, it can be supremely and mutually valuable to figure out a roadmap to having a loved one *know* you.

CHAPTER 20

Humility

—ɯ—

What the world needs is more geniuses with humility. There are so few of us left.
OSCAR LEVANT

My husband and I divorced over religious differences.He thought he was God, and I didn't.
?

To be ignorant of one's ignorance is the malady of the ignorant.
A. ALCO

The highest form of wisdom is kindness.
TALMUD

Some people are born on third base and go through life thinking they hit a triple.
BARRY SWITZER

It wasn't until late in life that I discovered
how easy it is to say "I don't know."
W. SOMERSET MAUGHAM

HUMILITY IS AN ESSENTIAL INGREDIENT to a harmonious marriage, and harmony leads to an easy marriage.

Humility is defined as a modest view of one's own importance. In contrast, arrogance is defined as an exaggerated view of one's importance. The repugnant synonyms for arrogance include: pompous, overbearing, egotistic and self-righteous.

No one has all the answers. No one is right all the time. For example, you could be a highly book-smart person on parenting, yet your parenting instincts may be no better than your spouse's.

A wise person is a humble person, and a wise person realizes how little they know. There are all types of situations in life that can be handled in different ways. Keep in mind that people are not stupid if they don't agree with you. With most things in a marriage, there is no one right way.

Even if your friends or employees think you're brilliant, don't be condescending to your spouse. Even if you supervise a hundred people on your job, you still need to take out the trash…without attitude.

Having a higher formal education than your spouse or making more money than your spouse are not valid reasons to feel superior to your spouse.

There are many times in life and many aspects of life in which wisdom is so much more valuable and supportive in a marriage than just being smart. Saying, "Well, you could do it this way or that way…" can be so much more pleasant than "You *have* to do it this way/You *should* do it this way/ You *must* do it this way."

CHAPTER 21

Honesty & Trust

—✷—

"Just be yourself" is actually bad
advice to some people.
BRUCE FRIEDIN

You are free to choose, but you are not
free to choose the consequences
of your choice.
?

We are all travelers in the wilderness of this world,
and the best we can find in our
travels is an honest friend.
ROBERT LOUIS STEVENSON

Just be honest with me or stay away from me.
It's not that difficult.
?

She totally trusted me at a time
when I was a dreadfully dishonest husband.
Now I'm a virtuous loving husband, and
she doesn't trust me at all.
?

Don't tell me what they said about me.
Tell me why they were so comfortable
to say it around you.
THE GODFATHER

AMONG THE GREATEST ASPECTS OF a good marriage are comfort and security. Just like the security you may feel when your primary care doctor tells you everything is fine at your checkup, it's wonderful to go through life feeling the security and comfort that your spouse is honest, loyal and trustworthy.

Similar to the shattering of security when one is told they have cancer, the security inherent in a marriage can be shattered with major betrayals.

If you have a first date who tells you s/he cheated on their last three spouses or partners, don't expect that person to be any different with you. Does the person you're dating tell you how they lie/cheat in business?

Even when dating, one may detect small lies. If someone is lying about trivial things, it may also suggest they have a problem with lying about the big things in life. It is a painful challenge to marry someone with a habit of lying.

Dishonesty is not exactly the same as lying. Dishonesty refers to deceitfulness and/or fraudulence, which can take other forms besides lying.

Should you discover in the course of your marriage that your partner has been dishonest or deceitful, you may not have any choice but to go for professional help together (assuming you don't seek a divorce).

Dishonesty is sometimes so ingrained into one's character, it can be extremely difficult to change. And, of course, people sometimes lie to their therapist.

Hyperbole is defined as exaggerations not to be taken seriously. People who speak with exaggeration can actually be quite entertaining (e.g., "I saw the funniest movie last night."). Although they can be great story-tellers, we know to listen to their stories with a "grain of salt."

Some people don't realize that exaggerations can be harmful, inflammatory and distracting. If you want to be taken seriously, you are advised not to exaggerate. Thus, instead of saying "You never take out the trash!' it's less inflammatory to say "Please take out the trash." And don't resort to the sarcastic "Can't you see the trash needs to be taken out?" This is not a matter of always "walking on eggs." It's a matter of being accountable for what you say.

Some people have a bad habit of saying what they think their spouse wants to hear. In other words, "I'll be home in ten minutes" really should be: "I'll probably be home in about a half hour."

Everyone has to say things their spouse doesn't want to hear. Better to deal with your spouse's annoyance than to be accused of being deceitful or irresponsible. Don't patronize your spouse by brushing them off.

Each person needs to be responsible for every word they say. If you say "Pick up some milk on the way home," you can't get angry if your spouse didn't get the container size you wanted. You should have been more specific.

If your wife asks for your opinion on what she's wearing, be honest but not hurtful. Saying "That outfit doesn't flatter you" isn't as nasty as "Your hips look huge." If your husband wants to go out with friends, don't tell him to go and then hold it against him.

Overall, taking a few extra seconds to say what you mean and mean what you say, goes a long way in life.

CHAPTER 22

Arguments

—∿—

No matter how thin the pancake,
it has two sides.
?

Lady Nancy Astor: If I were your wife, I'd
put poison in your coffee. Winston Churchill:
If I were your husband, I'd drink it.

Mary and I have been married 47 years,
and not once have we ever had an argument
serious enough to mention the word divorce.
Murder, yes; but divorce, never.
JACK BENNY

Often the difference between a successful marriage
and a mediocre one consists of
leaving about three or four things a day unsaid.
HARLAN MILLER

No man can think clearly when
his fists are clenched.
GEORGE NATHAN

SOME COUPLES GET DIVORCED BECAUSE they argue about: 1) almost everything; 2) one constant major issue; or 3) they never argue.

The art of the argument is critical to the safety, comfort and stability of a marriage. All types of large and small conflicts occur in the course of marriage. How you deal with conflict and how you argue determines the quality of your marriage. A single vicious act in an argument can lay the immediate foundation for a divorce.

By definition, an *argument* is an angry exchange of opposing views. A *disagreement,* or difference of opinion, may or may not involve anger. Ideally, anger is avoided in a disagreement.

There are many life situations involving disagreements or conflicts that should *not* lead to angry arguments. In order to avoid an argument, a disagreement needs time to be properly and patiently addressed.

Repeated arguments wear people down. Typically, a person argues with the goal of winning. But remember, if there is winning, there is losing. And no one wants to lose.

Anger easily escalates between spouses with words, exaggerations, nastiness and voice volume. Voice levels increase like a tennis match. Before they know it, and within seconds, spouses are hurting each other. This is so oppressive to a marriage. It's the total *opposite* of easy.

Disagreements need to be controlled in order to avoid arguments. Furthermore, disagreements need to move in a *linear* direction. Nothing is more frustrating than the feeling of *going around in circles* (i.e., not getting closure).

Don't keep saying the same thing. Don't bring up extraneous topics. Don't pretend you're listening. Always try to reach resolution and closure in a respectful way. You can almost always stop and restart the disagreement at another time.

Apologies are crucial to a good marriage. No healthy person wants to be married to someone who won't apologize.

No one is perfect. Everyone loses their temper at times. Everyone gets caught off guard at times and overreacts emotionally. But wrong is wrong, and when you know it, apologize for being nasty and hurtful…with no strings attached.

And no half-hearted apologies such as "I'm sorry if what I said hurt your feelings." Just say "I'm sorry for what I said."

Get professional help if you and your spouse seem to be arguing all the time. Get professional help if your arguments involve explosive outbursts, especially with violence or threats of violence.

Do not argue if one or both of you are even mildly intoxicated.

If you can imagine, some couples never argue. Is that a good thing? It depends. If people prevent anger from going to the surface, where is it then going? Unresolved anger can quietly erode the relationship. Silencing your anger can be extremely unhealthy not only for you but for your marriage.

CHAPTER 23

Anger, Part 1

—ᴍ—

Anybody can become angry, that is easy.
But to be angry with the right person,
and to the right degree, and at the right time,
and for the right purpose, and in
the right way, that is not within everybody's power.
That is not easy.
ARISTOTLE

All married couples should learn the art of battle
as they should learn the art of making love.
Good battle is objective and honest—
never vicious or cruel.
Good battle is healthy and constructive,
and brings to a marriage the
principle of equal partnership.
ANN LANDERS

*I first learned the concepts of nonviolence
in my marriage.*
M. GANDHI

*Never shout at each other unless
the house is on fire.*
?

Rule Number One:

NEVER HURT THE ONES YOU love. *Never* try to hurt your spouse in any way whatsoever, no matter how angry you are.

Rule Number Two:

No exceptions to Rule Number One.

Rule Numbers Three-Seven:

Never insult or humiliate your spouse.
  Never call each other hurtful names.
  Never embarrass your spouse. Never.
  Don't be a bully. No name-calling.
  No matter how angry you are, be respectful.

There are no exceptions to these rules. If you think there are exceptions, you shouldn't be married. A healthy person will not tolerate violations of these rules.

If you grew up with one or both parents with severe anger problems and/or alcoholism/addiction, you should seriously consider the benefits of obtaining individual psychotherapy even if you think you don't need it.

An alcoholic/addict parent causes a legacy of painful and long-lasting effects on all children into adulthood. All adults of alcoholic/addict parents should seek out self-understanding through therapy, AA support groups and/or readings as to how they may be manifesting unrealized problems.

If you suffer from: chronic irritability, internal tension, explosiveness, often feeling like your head is going to explode, grouchiness, often waking up angry, drinking and violence, road rage, chronic sullenness, chronic moodiness, volatile moods, chronic agitation, cyclic mood swings that last for days or weeks, angry outbursts in social situations—these are all indicators that something is wrong with you personally and not necessarily the marriage or your spouse.

Of course, chronic marital problems may lead to chronic anger problems. But one way or another, get help. If you think it's you, you should be professionally checked medically and psychologically.

CHAPTER 24

Anger, Part 2

—ᴠ—

I found my inner bitch and ran with her.
COURTNEY LOVE

Hurt people hurt people.
?

Oscar Wilde: "Do you mind if I smoke?"
Sarah Bernhardt: "I don't care if you burn."
The girl gave him a look which ought to have
stuck at least four inches out of his back.
RAYMOND CHANDLER

<u>Facts:</u>

* The angrier you get, the more irrational you get.
* The more irrational you get, the more you will exaggerate.
* The more you exaggerate, the more inflammatory your words will get.

87

- The angrier you get, the more defensive your spouse will get.

- The more upset you both become, the less productive the interaction between the two of you. It's a destructive waste.

- Do not try to have a discussion if one of you is too angry. An angry spouse doesn't have adequate patience or tolerance for the other one.

- An angry spouse wants to talk, not listen.

- The angrier you get, the more you will exaggerate the faults in your spouse or your criticisms of your spouse. This is useless and destructive. A savage waste.

- Do not exaggerate during a tense conversation. Be accurate with everything you say. Take your time and speak as quietly as possible. Loud voices provoke louder and louder reactions.

- Knowing when to be quiet and listen is just as critical as knowing when to speak.

- Just because you talk a lot doesn't mean you're a good communicator.

- Don't just blurt things out. Censor yourself in order not to make things worse.

WHEN YOU ARE ANGRY AND need to have a discussion about something serious, remember some reasons why psychotherapy and marriage counseling works. The format of psychotherapy is a superb role model for your discussions and disagreements at home:

- The therapist and patient(s) are sitting down and facing each other.
- They talk quietly. They listen carefully.
- They carefully choose their words in order for the other to accurately understand.
- It's okay if it gets emotional at times, as long as it's controlled.
- There's no TV on. There is no TV on mute. No texting.
- No taking phone calls.
- They are not in a moving car.
- They are not eating.
- They are not in a restaurant.
- They are not reading a newspaper nor having alcoholic drinks.
- They are not doing chores.
- There are no kids running around.

When you hear something vicious, you can't un-hear it. When you see something terrible, you can't un-see it. Things get said and done in anger which can ripple through a lifetime.

You are accountable for everything you say and do. You have a right get angry at your spouse; you don't have a right to be cruel or vicious.

Never threaten divorce when you are angry and hysterical. The time to discuss divorce is when you are calm and focused.

Keep in mind that you don't have to threaten divorce; you can say that you are thinking of divorce or that the marital problems are driving you closer to divorce. That's when you will be taken seriously.

Time alone does not heal *all* wounds, physical or psychological. Don't be hurtful.

CHAPTER 25

Cleansing Your Marriage of Passive-Aggressive Anger

—⚬⚬⚬—

*Never push a loyal person to the point
where they don't care.*
?

*Women are not moody.
We simply have days when we are
less inclined to put up with your shit.*
?

*Why are you so defensive?
I was only joking.*
?

PASSIVE REFERS TO UNEMOTIONAL AND undemonstrative. Aggressive refers to expressing hostility and likelihood of expressing anger or an attack. Put passive and aggressive together, and you have *camouflaged* expressions of anger.

Take the words "Nice shoes." Depending on your facial expression and tone of voice, it is either a compliment or a sarcastic remark. To say something complimentary along with a smirk is what is called passive-aggressive.

Saying you're angry is not passive-aggressive. Screaming in anger is not passive-aggressive. These are overt expressions of anger.

Being passive-aggressive is a way of *punishing* your spouse. Refusing sex can be passive-aggressive. Refusing to talk can be passive-aggressive. Spending too much money can be passive-aggressive. Denying you're angry can be passive-aggressive.

Habitual lateness to work is a way of showing disdain for the job. Willfully leaving messes for your spouse to clean up—knowing it upsets your spouse—is passive-aggressive. Keeping your arms down while being hugged can be passive-aggressive.

Passive-aggressiveness is "acting out" anger either verbally or behaviorally. It is a character trait in some people. Sometimes it occurs unconsciously; the person is not aware that they even have angry feelings. It can be grueling and exhausting to have to deal with chronic passive-aggressive hostility.

Playful sarcasm may have no intent to hurt your spouse, but there are many types of sarcastic comments that reflect anger or disgust (passive-aggressive). Furthermore, the spouse or relative who is always accusing you of being *too sensitive* to their sarcasm may well have unresolved anger and jealousy toward you which they cannot reveal.

At times, the first indication that your spouse is passive-aggressive is your own confusion. When you have to stop and ask yourself, "What did he mean by that?" or "Why is she taking so long to get ready to go to my parents?" the answer may be that your spouse is expressing angry resistance to you.

Chronic passive-aggressiveness makes a marriage very difficult. It wears down the spouse and the marriage. Conversely, being aware of your anger and constructively expressing it makes marriage much easier.

On a final note, if you want your spouse to be honest with you, s/he has to be able to express anger overtly, directly and productively. You don't want your spouse thinking that if would have been much easier if they lied.

CHAPTER 26

The Sigh & Eye-roll

—⟋⟋⟋—

Oops!
Did I just roll my eyes out loud?
?

A SIGH IS DEFINED AS a deep, audible breath expressing fatigue, relief or sadness. It is sometimes accompanied with a slouch of the shoulders. An eye-roll is basically an upward action of the eyes in disapproval or exasperation.

All things considered, the sigh and eye-roll are about the mildest forms of expressing disapproval. In many instances, they're neither aggressive nor passive aggressive reactions. Yet, in some marriages, these behaviors evoke extreme reactions of anger and resentment. But why?

Adults and children have a congenital capacity to express anger (from annoyance to rage). It's a core emotion. One of the most vital functions of being a parent is teaching your children acceptable and unacceptable expressions of anger as they grow up and become adults. In other words, don't teach your kids to not get angry; teach your kids *how* to be angry.

The following two examples illustrate common situations of spousal over-reactions to sighs and eye-rolls.

Example#1:
Him: "Do you want to go to a movie?"
Her: (Sigh and eye-roll) "Oh, alright."
Him: (Annoyed) "Forget it." (Walks away)

However, what if he ignored her negative reaction, they saw the movie, and she *loved* the movie?

Example #2:
Her: "Please take the trash out."
Him: (Sigh and eye-roll) (He proceeds to take out the trash.)
Her: "Why do you have to be so difficult? I do everything around here."

But wait…He didn't refuse. He didn't argue. He didn't accuse her of nagging. He sighed! That's it.

You cannot expect that everything you suggest and ask from your spouse should be met with his/her acceptance and a smile.

Plus, you shouldn't be that hypersensitive that you react with anger to very mild reactions of fatigue, exasperation or low motivation to do what you requested.

CHAPTER 27

Living Harmoniously
With a Narcissistic
Spouse

—ɯɯ—

That's enough of me talking about myself.
Let's hear you talk about me.
?

She has mirrors on the inside of her sunglasses.
?

When science discovers the center of the universe,
a lot of people will be disappointed to find
they are not in it.
BERNARD BAILY

Don't interrupt me while I'm insulting you.
?

As long as I get my way, I'm not hard to please.

?

THERE IS AN ENORMOUS AMOUNT of literature these days on the topics of narcissism, narcissistic spouses and growing up with narcissistic parents. This chapter focuses on the challenges and obstacles of having an easy marriage with a narcissistic spouse.

Some of the offensive narcissistic personality characteristics which cause an exceptionally difficult marriage include the following: extreme self-importance; difficulty feeling love toward others; selfishness; cravings for admiration; self-centeredness; a grandiose view of oneself; and inability to empathize or sympathize with others.

Additional characteristics include: hypersensitivity to imagined insults or criticisms; exaggeration of accomplishments; pretending to be more important or significant than they actually are; viewing children as trophies; emotionally distant; disliking others who don't admire them; contempt of others to make oneself feel more important; exploitation of others; unreasonable sense of entitlement; arrogance; potentially sadistic; shamelessness; and poor interpersonal boundaries.

In other words, this kind of person is problematic and difficult as a spouse, a parent and as a human being in general.

In terms of living with a narcissistic spouse, there are some recommendations which are offered herein which may help to make
marriage less difficult.

The most helpful suggestion is getting the spouse to understand
that their self-centeredness and sense of entitlement is extremely
hurtful and to get professional help from a psychotherapist who is
well versed in dealing with narcissism. This is a hard sell, however.

There are suggestions in the pop literature which more or
less, basically encourage you to give in and enable the narcissist
to have whatever s/he wants. That is not the approach I would
suggest.

Some narcissistic individuals have a sadistic side to their personality. That means they experience pleasure out of hurting and
dominating others. Accordingly, the provoked narcissist can be
very hurtful.

* Set boundaries that you're comfortable with and stay as
  firm as you can during conflict or verbal attacks.
* Make it clear that you are not at their beck and call.
* Make it clear that *not* arguing does *not* mean you agree
  with them. Arguing with a narcissist is often a waste of
  your time.
* Don't get lured into raising your voice and getting
  overheated.
* Trying to reason with a narcissist when they're raging is
  often fruitless.
* It can be a waste of your time to rage back at them.

* Make it clear that you have zero tolerance for being belittled or berated.
* Pick your battles and on your terms. Confront them when both of you are in a calm state.
* Sometimes you have to look for a hidden agenda to their manipulation. It may not be what it seems on the surface.
* Stand up to any attempt to shame you when your desires for closeness, romance or desires for sex are being ridiculed or trivialized. Do not tolerate and do not ignore being shamed or humiliated. Walk out of the room or get out of the car if necessary.
* Demanding humility and cooperation can be helpful. Many narcissists do not want to lose their marriages or families.

Part IV: Everyday Details

CHAPTER 28

Chores

*I could keep this kitchen clean if you people
would stop eating here.*
?

*My second favorite household chore is ironing.
My first being hitting my head
on the top bunk bed until I faint.*
ERMA BOMBECK

Life's too short to fold fitted sheets.
LISA QUINN

THE DISTRIBUTION OF CHORES IN a marriage has to be psycho-logically equitable. It has to be fair to each of you. But this doesn't mean the chores have to be 50/50.

People change and evolve during the course of life. What may feel equitable at ten years of marriage may feel unfair five years later. Plus, attitudes change toward who's doing what at home. Couples always need to have calm constructive talks about what they'd like to change—not raging, sarcastic or hysterical tantrums.

<u>Kids and Chores</u>
You don't need to pay your kids to do basic chores. Kids are part of your family. Chores build character in kids. Doing chores builds independence, confidence, pride, and competence. Money and bribes don't build character.

Kids can learn meal-making skills, shopping skills, home maintenance, laundry, and organizational skills. Even though kids can learn to do chores earlier than you might think, don't expect them to be adults. Don't expect your kids to think, act and feel as if they're mini-adults.

Having a short family meeting is a realistic way to explain to the kids what your new requests and expectancies are regarding chores. You and your spouse should decide the agenda before you sit down with the kids.

"Please pass the ketchup" is about the most unemotional, unembellished, practical request that a person can make. It is a pure, *matter-of-fact* request. It perfectly exemplifies the type of statements and requests that need to occur repeatedly in a marriage and with raising children of all ages.

As stated earlier, the angry and sarcastic "Can't you see the trash needs to be taken out?" should just be "Please take the trash out." The angry "Why is the TV so loud?" should just be the very simple "Please lower the TV."

Obviously, there are expectancies and obligations in a marriage. You shouldn't have to tell your spouse to go to work every day, and nor should you have to tell your spouse to wash the dishes every day.

When something needs to be done, always consider expressing yourself in a *matter-of-fact* way. It is civil and non-antagonistic.

It's noteworthy that when it comes to meals, there's the chore of preparing meals and the chore of *deciding* what dishes to have in a meal. You'd be surprised to know that some people have much more trouble deciding what to make than actually making the meal. In other words, the decision-making and coordination are a kind of (mental) labor in themselves. Such effort needs to be respected.

Most married couples would agree that the wife tends to be the *dispatcher* at home. She's the one who is likely to give household requests to her husband and kids.

Even though it may take less than two seconds to make a request, many women resent having to make the requests time and again. They want their husbands and kids to know what to do and to do it without reminders. This is very reasonable, yet it often doesn't happen.

Everyone should remember that forgetting to do a chore is not a catastrophe. It doesn't deserve a massive negative response.

If you want an easy marriage, you have to show effort, motivation and initiative toward the many responsibilities, big chores, little chores, and the cleaning up that is part of life and part of having a peaceful and harmonious marriage.

One shouldn't always wait to be reminded to complete chores.

CHAPTER 29

Clutter & Home Cleanliness

—✺—

I want to lead the Victorian life,
surrounded by exquisite clutter.
FREDDIE MERCURY

Organized clutter is still clutter.
CORIE CLARK

Get rid of clutter and you may just find it was
blocking the door you've been looking for.
KATRINA MAYER

YOU'RE AN ADULT AND YOU married an adult. And you should be living as equal adults.

Don't parent your spouse as if s/he's a child. Conversely, don't act like a child who wants and expects his/her parents to clean up your messes! In other words, don't be irresponsible and childlike.

Seriously, if you wanted to live like a child, marriage was not a good idea.

Clean up your own messes in the bathroom, kitchen, bedroom, and living room. Put your stuff away. Don't leave your stuff around for your spouse to clean up after you.

Don't leave messes in the sink for someone else to clean up. Don't leave laundry baskets of clothes in the bedroom. Don't leave half-filled glasses or soda cans around the house.

Messes and piles of stuff are not sexy. Huge piles of old mail and catalogs are nasty and unhealthy. Messes can be forms of disrespect. And even if you don't mean disrespect, your spouse will experience your mess as disrespect.

Being compulsive with cleaning doesn't mean you have a disorder (viz., obsessive-compulsive *disorder*). Wanting a non-cluttered home doesn't mean you have some type of pathology.

But becoming enraged over a fork in the sink or complaining about how the towels have to be perfectly folded can be very unreasonable. Remember: *It ain't cancer!*

You knew what each other were like before you married each other. So, expecting the other to dramatically change after marriage is unreasonable. However, you can and should compromise with each other. I cannot emphasize enough how important it is show *good will* in a marriage.

Entering a Japanese styled garden tends to produce an effect of tranquility almost immediately. It is configured with Zen concepts. Everything is precisely organized, pristine and immaculate. Nothing is out of order. Sand. Rocks. Manicured evergreens. Trickling water from a fountain. Perfect order.

The point is that *order produces calmness* for most people. Disorder produces tension and unrest. This concept applies to one's home environment.

Clutter can be a health problem. It overloads your senses. It leads to feelings of being overwhelmed. Procrastination of decluttering can also cause marital conflict and moderate to severe resentment.

CHAPTER 30

Finances

Marriage is about love.
Divorce is about money.
?

I think men who have a pierced ear
are better prepared for marriage.
They've experienced pain and bought jewelry.
RITA RUDNER

I like long romantic walks to the bank.
?

THERE IS NO ONE PERFECT way to manage the finances for all marriages. Merging incomes and debts need to be carefully and honestly evaluated *well before* marriage.

Regardless of your financial system, it is essential to have a harmonious system of accounting, bookkeeping, communication about finances, and a bill payment system. Some people prefer separate checking accounts; some prefer a joint account. Whatever makes you happy and compatible.

Given that the rule of thumb is that whomever pays the bills will have the highest stress, it's important to appreciate the efforts of the bill-payer. When the bill-payer wants to have a discussion with you, it is advisable to be patient, turn off the TV, and have a conversation.

Household finances is a set of stressful issues for most marriages of all economic levels. Respect needs to be shown to the spouse who balances the checkbook and juggles the bills.

I highly recommend that for most marriages, there needs to be regular communication and transparency about the finances. No one should hide credit card statements. No secret credit cards or secret checking accounts. No secret vacation funds. No secret Christmas funds.

Don't live with your head in the sand, oblivious to what your joint income is and how the income is being spent. Your income should not be a secret.

Always make sure that you are both in a calm frame of mind when you are discussing finances, bills, investments, long-term financial planning, large gifts for your children, emergency funds and significant purchases.

It is perfectly reasonable and often necessary to have repeated conversations about one financial topic before you reach resolution. Stay calm. No yelling or raised voices. It's okay to take a break to calm down.

You should be able to know what each of you earns in income. You should know whether there is credit card debt, alimony obligations, and student loan debt before you get married.

Conflict and tension can emerge in a marriage whether both are employed, one is employed, or neither is employed. A couple making a very good combined income can run into lots of serious concerns when one stops working (such as with having children). Many changes may occur which need to be carefully analyzed and discussed.

It can't be emphasized enough how vital it is to have patient and constructive conversations about current and future financial issues regarding expenses, desires, budgets, priorities, and costs.

CHAPTER 31

Gift-Giving

—∿—

Life is short; buy the shoes.
?

It's not a matter of what you spend.
It's a matter of what you save.
?

I have the simplest tastes.
I am always satisfied with the best.
OSCAR WILDE

Q: Do you buy each other gifts for special occasions such as birthdays?
A: No. We are mature adults.

DON'T CLAIM THAT YOU DON'T have time to shop or that you don't know what to buy for your spouse. It's a lame excuse, and no one believes it.

If your partner has made it clear s/he loves greeting cards, just buy them. Don't complain, and don't politicize the greeting card industry. It doesn't hurt to be *generous of spirit.*

Don't agree to *not* buy gifts for special occasions. Why be so dull? Your marriage isn't worth gifts? Really?

You're not that busy or that important that you can't schedule some time to shop for a gift—in stores or online. Don't dumb down your marriage.

Don't wake up on Mother's Day and ask your wife, "So what do you wanna do today?" Make a plan ahead of time.

Don't use a birthday or anniversary to buy a gift for "the house."

Teach your children at an early age to show their love and appreciation by making cards or shopping with you for gifts. Having a special family meal is one way to acknowledge your spouse is important to you.

Put some effort into looking for gifts that your spouse will enjoy personally. Buy or even make something (such as framing a photo) that implies "I want you to be happy, and I'm happy if you're happy."

When gift selection becomes a futile chore because of frequent rejections, I suggest that you shop together. Plan some time to spend a few hours shopping together for gifts. Make the most of it. Make it a date. Have some fun.

CHAPTER 32

Grooming & Hygiene

—ɰ—

She has lilacs for pubic hair.
BLAKE EDWARDS ON HIS
WIFE JULIE ANDREWS

*Simplicity, good taste, and grooming
are the three fundamentals of good dressing
and these do not cost money.*
CHRISTIAN DIOR

*A girl should be two things:
who and what she wants.*
COCO CHANEL

It costs a lot of money to look this cheap.
DOLLY PARTON

My hair was famous before I was.
CHRISTOPHER WALKEN

GROOMING AND HYGIENE ARE NOT topics to be trivialized or dismissed. Romance and sex appeal partially depend on physical attributes, aesthetics and presentation.

Keep in mind that beauty and sex appeal are completely different. There are beautiful women with no sex appeal, and homelier women with great sex appeal. Similarly, there are handsome men who present with no sex appeal, and much less handsome men who present themselves with very interesting appeal.

Are you a woman who wears old, floppy sweatsuits most of the time? Do you only put on makeup when you go to work or weddings? Do you care if your hairstyle is appealing to your husband? Do you think you're not supposed to care?

Are you a guy who puts on the same tattered, baseball t-shirt you've had for 20 years? Do you wear 10 year old underwear? Do you only shave on days you go to work? Do you wear button-down shirts that look as if the buttons around your abdomen will pop off any second? Do you think you're not supposed to care?

Do either of you leave the bathroom door open when you urinate or defecate, thinking that your spouse just loves to hear the beautiful sound of your body functions? Do you freely burp and fart in front of each other?

Do you wear blue jeans and sneakers seven days a week including Saturday nights? Do you justify this by claiming your first amendment civil rights to look any way you want?

Do you wear stained shirts around each other?

Everyone has the prerogative to have any kind of marriage they want. But if you want affection and sex in your marriage, you have to have some understanding about how sex appeal works. Pride in appearance is sexy.

Don't think that you can look and smell anyway you want and your spouse will have a desire to kiss you, let alone want to have sex with you. Or even be in the same room with you.

Grooming and hygiene have a very important role in sex appeal. Here are some factors you shouldn't overlook: dental hygiene, breath, hair style, body odor, choice of clothing, cleanliness of self, cleanliness of clothing, what you wear to bed at night, and table manners. Yes, table manners.

Considering that you spend about one third of your life in your bedroom, evaluate what you wear to bed. Take a good look at yourself at bedtime. Would you like to sleep next to you? Does your sleepwear say, "Stay away from me?"

Most people put effort into their appearance when they first date each other. Why stop after marriage?

CHAPTER 33

Hobbies

—ııı—

*It can be coins or sports or politics or horses or
music or faith... the saddest people I've ever
met in life are the ones who don't care deeply
about anything at all. Passion and satisfaction
go hand in hand, and without them,
any happiness is only temporary,
because there's nothing to make it last.*
NICHOLAS SPARKS

*Hobbies are not just for young
children or the elderly.*
BRUCE FRIEDIN

A HOBBY IS WHAT YOU do for fun. You enjoy it by yourself, with
friends, other couples, or with your spouse. Hobbies are inherently pleasurable. But they also allow you to get your mind off the
serious and problematic parts of your life.

It's completely unjustifiable for you to think you don't have time for a hobby. A hobby can be enjoyed occasionally or frequently. There are no rules as to how often one should partake in hobbies. It's important for your children to know that you participate in hobbies. Hobbies give you and your spouse topics to casually discuss for pleasure.

Of the couples who go into therapy because they have lost the romance and sex in their marriage, it is often the case that they also don't take any time for the pursuit of pleasurable activities. This is what can be referred to as a *systemic* issue.

Everything in their life is work, kids, house. They're one hundred percent responsible, 24/7. No time set aside for lighthearted activities. Guess what happens, sooner or later?

Walking the dog is not a hobby. For most people, going to a gym is not a hobby either. If you and your spouse don't have any hobbies, take a step back and think about it. Why are you beneath having hobbies? Why is it wrong to have a hobby? Why are you going through life like this?

Go online or to a local bookstore and do some investigating about possible hobbies. Sprinkle your married life with hobbies. They're refreshing and revitalizing.

CHAPTER 34

In-laws

—ᴖᴖ—

Everyone has heard at least one
mother-in-law joke.
How many can remember a father-in-law joke?
JUDY ALLEN

Families are like fudge—
mostly sweet with a few nuts.
?

EVERYONE HAS THEIR LIMITATIONS WITH everything in life, including how much time to spend with relatives, whether yours or
your spouse's.

Do not force your family—no matter how sweet and generous
they are—on your spouse. If you're getting pressure to be with
your parents *every* Sunday for dinner—be careful with how you

handle this. Compromise is often necessary to maintain a nice harmony with your spouse.

Let's face it—everyone has relatives they would not spend time with on holidays if it wasn't *mandatory.*

Boundaries are the key issue here. It's not a good idea to let your parents dictate how you should lead your life. You and your spouse are adults—just like your parents!

Some parents and in-laws are very demanding. Try not to be bullied by them. If you have severe guilt and difficulty tolerating their disapproval of you, you may be a candidate for professional help.

Some things are open to negotiation with relatives and some things aren't. Sooner or later, one needs to be assertive with in-laws.

As an adult, you should be able to speak directly or express grievances to your parents and your in-laws. Communication with your in-laws doesn't need to go through your spouse all the time.

Do you really need to go to every relative's birthday party? Do you really need to be there the entire time? Or can you stop by for just a little while? Negotiations with your spouse should be calm and respectful. Don't expect to always get your way. Bad-mouthing your spouse's family can cause very serious rifts in your marriage.

Some people are closer with the in-laws than their own family. Some people don't have in-laws. Remember, "family isn't everything," in a family with major dysfunctions and outright nasty relatives.

Relationships with in-laws are like other relationships in some ways. It's not unusual to get on each other's nerves. As with all relationships, sometimes you just have to sit down, and talk things out.

CHAPTER 35

Mealtimes &
Meal Planning

—◊◊◊—

She didn't know how to make a wild duck,
but she could certainly take a
tame one and aggravate it.
?

All great change in America begins
at the dinner table.
RONALD REAGAN

THIS PART OF MARRIAGE AND lifestyle is often overlooked as having a significant role in the happiness of a marriage. But it does play a major role!

The communication about food and meals needs to be easy and non-complicated. Simple and brief conversations about meals should be a matter-of-fact routine.

Don't minimize the value of having enjoyable meal experiences. Throughout all cultures, meals are a vital and nurturing center-piece of marriage and family.

Among the most common problems pertaining to meals:

Leaving messes for others to clean up.
* Unwillingness to help with meal preparation.
* Boring conversation.
* No conversation.
* Eating meals together while watching television or texting.
* Not expressing appreciation to whomever did the meal preparation.
* Unwillingness to participate in meal *planning*.
* Eating in a sloppy environment.
* Lack of hygiene/lack of manners.
* Being overly critical.
* Dull and lackluster meals.
* Yelling, criticisms and arguments at meals.
* Always eating with the kids and not as a couple.
* Never taking the time to have a romantic meal.
* Trying to make everyone happy with different meals at one sitting.
* A dirty, messy kitchen and table.

There are websites that refer to "conversation starters." This can be quite helpful to creating mealtime conversation for families.

For example, at dinner, one family member picks a starter topic out of a hat. The family can then have a decent and potentially interesting conversation. This can be a lot more enjoyable and interesting than "How was your day?"

Don't be afraid to require your kids to help with meal preparation. The younger you start your kids with this, it becomes their norm for years.

If putting a meal together always seems like torture, you need to understand why. Perhaps there was something about your childhood that's preventing you from nurturing your family. Perhaps you're disorganized and overwhelmed.

The value of occasional romantic meals with your spouse at home or in restaurants should never be underestimated. So what constitutes *romantic,* you ask? Not fast food (unless it's with champagne!). Soft lighting. Slow pace. Well-prepared food. Not plastic forks. Nicely served food. No TV or social media allowed at the table. Not taking phone calls. No kids. Nice atmosphere can be anything from at home or by the beach. Good conversation. And, hopefully, a few laughs.

CHAPTER 36

The Myth of Mr./Mrs. Flexible

—✺—

You have your way. I have my way.
As for the right way, the correct
way, and the only way,
it does not exist.
F. NIETZSCHE

Her: What do you want for dinner?
   Him: I don't care.

Her: What movie do you want to see?
   Him: I'm easy. Whatever you want.

Her: What should I wear to the party?
   Him: Whatever you want.

Her: What color should we paint the bedroom?
   Him: It doesn't matter to me.

Her: Where do you want to go on vacation?"
  Him: Whatever makes you happy.

Obviously, flexibility is an essential ingredient of a good marriage. Conversely, rigidity is a marriage killer. But for some people, what is purported to be flexibility is really something else.

In the above example, Mr. Flexible thinks he's a real easygoing guy. He thinks he's cooperative and flexible and doesn't make waves.

Well, guess what—Mr. Flexible is really Mr. Rigid. He's not flexible. It's the opposite! He's stubbornly not participating in his marriage and nor is he bringing any interest or excitement to the marriage.

Mr. Flexible is often Mr. Dud. In fact, Mr. Flexible may really be Mr. Passive-aggressive.

The issue is that it's important to participate in many choices and decisions involving the lifestyle of you and your spouse. It's very unappealing and somewhat of a dumbing down of your marriage when you don't express preferences.

Always deferring to your spouse is a way of being unconcerned about the quality of your marriage. Saying "whatever you want" can be like saying: *Your question is not important enough for me to spend even five seconds thinking about it.*

My final note is that decision-making is a type of work involving mental effort. When two people join in the process, it has the potential for the decision making to be an easier process. Of course, the process will always be more difficult when both spouses are stubborn or uncompromising.

CHAPTER 37

Parenting

—ɯ—

We have two wonderful children.
And another one.
BRIAN REGAN

My mother protected me from the world,
and my father threatened me with it.
QUENTIN CRISP

Don't limit your children to your own learning.
They were born in another time.
RABINIC SAYING

Educate your children to be happy, not rich.
That way they will know the value of things.
?

When you're teaching your children,
you're teaching your grandchildren.
?

*Not to teach your son to work is like
teaching him to steal.*
Talmud

*The way you talk to your children
is what becomes their own inner voice later in life.*
?

*When you're at a frustration point where you want
to strangle your teenager, just do the opposite.
Take him/her out to a relaxing dinner instead.
Just the two of you.*
Bruce Friedin

*Don't worry that children never listen to you;
worry that they are always watching you.*
Robert Fulghum

*A parent can only be as happy as his/her
least happy child.*
?

*As a child, my family's menu
consisted of two choices:
take it, or leave it.*
Buddy Hackett

*Ask your child what he wants for dinner only
if he's buying.*
FRAN LEBOWITZ

ALTHOUGH THIS IS NEITHER A parenting book nor a child development book, I can offer some advice based on common child and adolescent concerns and problems that arise in couples therapy sessions.

A variety of guidelines:

- Don't believe everything you read about kids, education, and parenting. Even so-called experts disagree with each other.
- Don't think your child's teachers have all the answers.
- A child growing up in a poor family can just as easily be spoiled as a child growing up in wealthy family.
- A child growing up with love in a poor home with well-adjusted parents is likely to be happier than a child growing up in a wealthy home with miserable parents.
- Never use shame, humiliation or embarrassment as a method of motivating your child to do well in any endeavor.

- Don't teach your children the limerick of "sticks and stones." It's completely untrue. Spiteful and humiliating words to a child can be painfully remembered for a lifetime.

- Adults shouldn't assume that their own parents loved them just because their parents had jobs. Being employed doesn't mean you love your kids.
- Don't make excuses for your own parents by saying they're from the *old country*. What old country? Peru? Tibet? Finland?
- Dinner conversation with the family on a daily basis can include telling each child: "Tell us one thing you learned in school today."

Raising children automatically involves repetition. Repetition of requests, instructions and reminders. The vast majority of these interactions should be with a matter-of-fact tone of voice. No screaming. Avoid getting frantic or rageful.

Consider this: if your children only respond to your instructions when you scream at them, maybe it means you have trained them to ignore you unless you scream at them.

Family meals are valuable opportunities to enjoy and bond. It seems increasingly common for families to not eat even one meal at home together. Always try to plan family meals—whether a couple of dinners per week or at least one weekend breakfast. And *no* television! And no video games. And no cell phones brought to the table. Don't be an emotionally crippled family that has to be entertained by electronics constantly.

Here's what I believe your children *should* experience from your marriage:

- That you laugh together.
- That you show affection to each other.
- That you each have hobbies.
- That you go out with your friends to have fun.
- That you go out with other couples to have fun.
- That you go out together.
- That you sit down, without distractions, in order to have serious conversations.
- That you are good listeners.

- That sometimes you lock your bedroom door.
- That you don't have the answers to everything.
- That you treat each other with respect, even when angry.
- That you treat your home with respect.
- That you treat the environment with respect.
- That you sometimes have interesting conversations.
- That you seek help for serious problems.
- That you're careful with your health.
- That you're happy for each other's successes and accomplishments.
- That you have a strong work ethic.
- That you help and support each other.
- That your anger is reasonable and not hurtful or abusive.
- That you don't abuse alcohol or drugs.
- That you don't humiliate each other.

CHAPTER 38

PMS

—⬯—

Women complain about PMS.
But I think of it as the only time of the month
when I can be myself.
Roseanne Barr

Do you know why they call it 'PMS'?
Because 'Mad Cow Disease' was already taken.
?

When women are depressed,
they eat or go shopping.
Men invade another country.
It's a whole different way of thinking.
Elayne Boosler

If women ran the world we wouldn't have wars;
just intense negotiations every 28 days.
Robin Williams

SOME MARRIED COUPLES HAVE THEIR worst arguments when the wife is having PMS—and neither of them realizes it.

PMS is a legitimate problem. It can cause so much physical turmoil within a woman that it can domino into irrational anger at her husband and/or at one of more of her children.

One of my physician friends calls it "hormotional" (the wallop from the interaction of hormones and emotions). There aren't many options for the treatment of PMS. Some physicians prescribe antidepressant medications.

Oil of primrose capsules does help some women while in the throes of PMS. It's considered a nutritional supplement. I discovered this recommendation in a very old nutrition book, and it has been very helpful to countless women. Always do some research before taking any supplements.

I suggest that husbands get a phone application that will notify them when their wife is due to become premenstrual. It definitely makes life easier.

Part V:
Easy Sex

*In my sex fantasy, nobody ever
loves me for my mind.*
Nora Ephron

A GOOD SEXUAL RELATIONSHIP IS an *easy* sexual relationship.

The more difficult a sexual relationship is, the more unpleasant and awkward it is and vice versa. Furthermore, difficult sex eventually leads to a domino effect of loss of desire, avoidance of sex, and /or sexual dysfunctions.

It's essential that you and your partner be able to discuss sex in terms of what's enjoyable and what's unenjoyable. What you like and don't like. What's exciting and what's boring. What feels good and what feels bad.

The moments right after sex can be a nice time to make comments as to what was pleasurable or for just being light-hearted. But issues and problems with sex need to be addressed in a sit-down situation at a different time. No nasty comments or criticisms right after sex. First thing is to calm down and gather your thoughts.

Whenever possible, try to discuss sex issues with an upbeat tone. At times, rather than expressing complaints per se, you may be able to discuss what you want to be different about sex.

Don't try to discuss too many problems in one conversation; it can be very disheartening. Perhaps a week or month later, have a little follow-up discussion as to whether the changes have been noticed and whether they are working out.

There are different aspects of sex which absolutely need to be easy: sexual advances, preparation, contraception, intercourse positions, length of sexual encounter, and the use of medications to enhance sexual functioning.

Although very little time in a marriage is spent having sex, it can play a huge role in a marriage. Not only do problems outside the bedroom ripple into the bedroom, but problems in the bedroom ripple into the rest of the marriage. Many sexual frustrations can be avoided or addressed properly when you know how.

CHAPTER 39

Sex & Aging

—∿∿—

I'm at the age where food has taken the place of sex
in my life. In fact, I've just had a mirror
put over my kitchen table.
RODNEY DANGERFIELD

When people ask me how old I am, I say:
"Age is just a number, and mine is unlisted."
?

IF YOU ASKED THE AVERAGE 20 year old married guy whether he'd prefer having 'good' sex five days a week or 'great' sex once a week, he would likely choose quantity. He has that preference because he doesn't yet know the differences between average sex and great sex. To him, all sex can seem great.

But what about the average 40 year old, married guy who's given that choice? Many middle age and older guys know the differences between average sex and great sex. That's when quality gets priority over quantity.

How about the 20 year old woman compared to the 40 year old woman? My opinion is that this is more complex. Young women are so much more informed about sexuality than previous generations of women. This has created an openness and willingness to seek sexual pleasure.

Nevertheless, young married women are having anywhere from terrible sex to great sex. Young or not young, I believe the majority of women are more likely to prefer great sex rather than average sex.

Married women lose their patience and tolerance for unpleasant or difficult sex as they get older. Bad or uninspiring sex gets tedious. Why bother?

The assumption of many marriage-avoidant people is that a sexual relationship automatically fades away in marriage. I have no problem arguing that quantity preferences fade over the long term, but not necessarily quality. In fact, the quality of sex in a marriage can get better over time.

Many years ago, I read an interview with a gay male porn star. At the time, the guy was in a monogamous relationship—this after many hundreds of prior sexual partners. The interviewer asked: "What's the difference for you between having had sex one time with hundreds of new partners compared to sex with only one person all the time?" I loved his answer: "Sex with someone brand new is always *more exciting* than with someone you've been with a long time. But sex with someone you've been with a long time is *better*."

Now, pause and think about that comment. *Exciting*, compared to *better*? At first, it seems like a contradiction. But it isn't. Some couples over time develop a very intimate and very satisfying sexual relationship. It gets better. Ideally, it stays exciting.

Sex with a new partner, however, causes some people to be self-conscious, anxious, and guarded. The sex can be exciting but awkward, difficult and/or dysfunctional.

There *is* a difference between exciting and better. Marital sex doesn't have to be difficult, bad or dull.

It's not just our physical bodies that age. Our marriage ages. And we age psychologically. Our desires age.

Just remember, sex will not become more enjoyable if you don't address what's bothering you.

CHAPTER 40

Sex & Male Aging

—ƚ₥—

A man is only as old as the woman he feels.
GROUCHO MARX

*Her: My gynecologist says I can't
have sex for two weeks.
Him: What did your dentist say?*
?

I'm an alpha male on beta blockers.
GEORGE CARLIN

THROUGHOUT THE LIFE SPAN OF all men, there are gradual changes in sexual functioning. This is universal, and there are no exceptions. What varies is when and how fast the changes occur. Adjustments can almost always be made to maintain an easy sexual relationship.

Most men and women are not well-informed as to what these gradual changes are. Gathering information can be very helpful toward staying ahead of these changes and not misinterpreting them.

<u>The age-related changes include:</u>

- Taking longer to get an erection.
- Requiring longer periods of psychological and physical stimulation to get an erection.
- Erections fluctuate more easily during sexual encounters.
- The amount of semen that's ejaculated decreases.
- The angle of erection goes from pointing upward to pointing downward.
- The force of ejaculation diminishes.
- Less intense orgasms.
- Softer erections.
- Complete erection may not occur until right before orgasm.
- Penis returns to relaxed state faster after orgasm.
- Longer periods between orgasm and the next desire for sex.

CHAPTER 41

Sex & Female Aging

—⟊⟊—

I'm afraid I can't go.
I've already taken off my bra,
so I'm in for the night.
?

Ten men waiting for me at the door?
Send one of them home.
I'm tired.
MAE WEST

THE MORE YOU KNOW ABOUT the basics of sex and aging, the more you can adjust to these factors without getting upset and frustrated. The prospect of getting upset (i.e., angry, embarrassed, anxious, guilty) with sex becomes a huge deterrent to sex. Again, sex can and should be easy at all ages.

To begin with, postmenopausal women produce less estrogen and testosterone. This tends to interfere with the vaginal lubrication process and vasocongestion of the vagina (relating to sexual arousal).

The vagina also tends to become less *elastic*. The normal age-related lessening of these hormones tends to cause less sexual desire. As a result of the loss of estrogen with age and menopause, the vaginal walls become thinner.

The vagina is the canal part of a woman's genitals. The vulva is the outside of the genitals: the urethra, clitoris, and the labia majora and labia minora (the *lips to the vagina).*

The vulva doesn't change much even into the early years of menopause. It tends to lose fullness, sooner or later, after menopause.

Burning and itching complaints are not uncommon in older women—potentially during exercise and vaginal stimulation. Burning is not uncommon with intercourse.

It is generally believed that regular sexual activity helps the vagina to stay flexible and moist.

Couples need to understand the categories of lubricants. There are over-the-counter lubricants and prescription hormone lubricants. Over-the-counter lubricants may not be helpful for the postmenopausal woman.

Over-the-counter lubricants include: water-based, silicone-based, oil-based and water plus silicone based. Glycerin is added to some water-based lubricants. Glycerin can be vegetable-based or synthetic. There are educational websites that explain the differences among lubricants and what might work best for you and your desires.

Hormone therapy (viz., the prescription lubricants) may help relieve vaginal dryness. Estrogen creams applied into the vagina may enhance blood flow to the vaginal area. It can facilitate both sensation and lubrication. You should know there are several formats for taking vaginal estrogen.

It is perfectly normal that as women age and their marriages age, they may need more stimulation, psychologically and physically, to become aroused. There may or may not be fewer muscle contractions during orgasm, which may result in less intense orgasms.

Women, more so than men, are likely to be increasingly self-conscious and critical of their bodies with age. Both sexes are impacted with gray hair, stretch marks, surgical scars and loss of muscle tone.

It is totally normal to be increasingly shy regarding total nakedness with sex. Therefore, modesty is a helpful factor in facilitating comfort and likelihood of arousal. If wearing attractive clothing during sex allows for loss of inhibitions and self-consciousness, go for it.

CHAPTER 42

Sexual Affection

—m—

I Wanna Hold Your Hand...Perhaps the most
f**king brilliant song ever written...they nailed it.
That's what everyone wants. Not 24-7 hot wet sex.
Not a marriage that lasts a hundred years.
No. They wanna hold your hand.
RACHEL COHN

I love firm hugs.
Statues are so affectionate.
Well, at least compared to my ex-wife.
JAROD KINTZ

We can live without religion and meditation,
but we cannot survive without human affection.
DALAI LAMA

SEXUAL AFFECTION CAN BE ONE of the most enjoyable aspects of marriage. Sexual affection doesn't just have to lead to sex. Sexual affection is an end in itself.

Sexual affection can also be thought of as romantic affection: flirting, kissing, touching, caressing, fondling, massaging, embracing, snuggling and playful talk.

In a good marriage, sexual affection makes people feel good about themselves, each other, and the marriage. It adds a sexy flair to the marriage. It keeps people feeling sexy and the marriage vibrant.

The lack of sexual affection can cause people to feel sexually and emotionally paralyzed.

In problematic/bad marriages, men and women don't want to be affectionate and they don't want their spouse to be affectionate. The lack of affection is a major red flag.

The chronic lack of playful sexual affection should be discussed and addressed because it can be a symptom of underlying marriage problems. It can also be a symptom of physical problems such as hormone imbalances. Remember, hormones do drive desires for affection and sex.

Another potential problem is obnoxious sexual affection. Both spouses should be sensitive to each other's likes and dislikes. Being sensitive should not be considered work. If your spouse doesn't want to be groped, pay attention. If your spouse is offended by your choice of words, pay attention and be cooperative. If a brief massage helps a spouse to be amorous, pay attention.

A very common problem is how couples deal with sexual arousal caused by affection. It's always unfortunate when a wife holds back from romantic affection because of how quickly her husband becomes aroused and then wants sex.

Some women will eventually refrain from being playful because if her husband sexualizes the affection and she rejects his sexual advance, he then becomes angry. And then she feels guilty. Then she feels angry. Now they're both upset.

In a sense, neither of them are wrong. She's not wrong for being playful. He's not wrong for getting aroused. So what should they do? Well, sometimes it helps for her to preface her playfulness that she just wants to be playful. That becomes the cue that, for whatever reason, she's not in the mood for sex.

CHAPTER 43

Foreplay

—⟋⟍—

*A dress makes no sense unless it inspires men
to want to take it off of you.*
FRANCOISE SAGAN

*You may know where to touch her,
but that doesn't mean you know how to touch her.
Take time to learn what she truly desires."*
STEPHAN LABOSSIERE

*The way a man is in bed indicates
how he feels about the universe.*
SUZY CHAFFEE

*For women the best aphrodisiacs are words.
The G-spot is in the ears.*
ISABEL ALLENDE

*She lowered her lashes until they almost cuddled
her cheeks and slowly raised them again, like
a theatre curtain. I was to get to know that
trick. That was supposed to make me roll over
on my back with all four paws in the air.*
RAYMOND CHANDLER

TO MOST PEOPLE, FOREPLAY IS the kissing, hugging, fondling, caressing, touching and oral sex which occurs before intercourse.

Some people prefer no foreplay. Some prefer extensive foreplay. The only guideline that matters is what makes two people happy.

What most men and many women don't realize nor appreciate is that foreplay can begin before you get in bed. Foreplay can be psychological.

Foreplay can begin hours before sex, such as: being at a party; having a nice dinner together; watching an entertaining TV show; or having a drink together.

When a husband says *"I have to work on her to get her aroused,"* there may be a chance she's not communicating what excites her or bores her. Or he could be too focused on getting her aroused from physical stimulation rather than psychological stimulation.

Perhaps she's not telling him that she knows she has no interest in sex right then. Or perhaps he's doing what she always tells him *not* to do. Or perhaps she can't get her mind off of something that has nothing to do with sex. Or perhaps he has bad breath

Be aware that as people age, the length and quality of foreplay becomes increasingly important to good sex. What worked at 30 may not work at 50. Or, you may just need a lot more of it. Or, you may want less of it.

There are three types of sexual stimulation: *psychological* (such as memories or fantasies; watching a sexually stimulating movie, viewing sexual photographs; reading sexually explicit stories; sex talk with your partner); *non-genital, physical stimulation*: kissing, touching, fondling, caressing, and massaging; and *genital stimulation* which consists of actual physical stimulation of the genitals.

The ability to get an erection from only psychological stimulation is gradually lost throughout the lifespan. The ability to get an erection from just non-genital stimulation is also gradually lost throughout life. Later in life, increasing amounts of direct penile stimulation are required in order to obtain an erection.

CHAPTER 44

Sexual Appetites & Preferences

—⁓—

Sex appeal is fifty percent what you've got and fifty percent what people think you've got.
SOPHIA LOREN

The human body is not a religious shrine. It's a pleasure palace.
BRUCE FRIEDIN

You don't appreciate a lot of stuff in school until you get older.
Little things like being spanked every day by a middle aged woman:
Stuff you pay good money for in later life.
EMO PHILIPS

I used to be Snow White, but I drifted.
MAE WEST

It's erotic if you're using a feather.
It's kinky if you're using the whole damn chicken.
?

The closest Charlotte had ever come to
getting screwed on a plane was the time
she lost all of her luggage on a
flight to Palm Beach.
?

If you use the electric vibrator near water,
you will come and go at the same time.
LOUISE SAMMONS

IDEALLY, A MARRIED COUPLE PRETTY much knows what each other's sexual preferences are before marriage. Unfortunately, however, there are some people who hide their real desires. Sooner or later, this is a problem.

Preferences refer to the variety of sexual factors which people learn through life experience, beginning early in life. For example, many adults are attracted to a type of person who resembles someone from their youth (such as a teacher or celebrity) with whom they had an attraction toward.

These learned preferences are acquired and involved in: sexual activities; sexual positions; sexy garments; physical attributes; role playing; dominance/submission.

Some couples prefer to have the same sexual experience every time. If it makes them both happy, no problem. Some couples prefer lots of variety with their sexual relationship. If it makes them happy, no problem.

As you can imagine, problems will occur when spouses have different desires, hopes and expectancies with their sexual relationship. Unfortunately, sexual compromise doesn't always happen.

When one spouse essentially says, "I don't like it and I don't want to learn to like it," there's not much to negotiate.

You both don't have to have the same level of desire for sexual activities. You can participate in some sexual activities out of good will—as long as there is no discomfort or resentment.

Some couples delve into the edgier or kinkier sexual areas just by talking about it during encounters. They would never do what they're fantasizing about, but the raunchy sex talk can be enjoyable and not dangerous to the relationship.

That said, people need to be very careful about revealing what or who they fantasize about. They should also be very selective about what they reveal about prior sexual experiences and relationships. It's a slippery slope. Sex talk fantasies about a celebrity is not as dangerous as revealing a fantasy about the neighbor.

I always advocate against any type of sexually open marriage. Having other sexual partners is very dangerous to a marriage.

Unexpected disasters can happen. Basically, when you play with fire, you will likely get very burned.

Overall, remember that being sexual is about sharing pleasure. *Giving* pleasure and *receiving* pleasure. As I often express to couples, good sex is about being 50 percent *selfless* and 50 percent *selfish*.

CHAPTER 45

Spontaneous Sex Versus Planning Sex

—⟋⟍—

No smoking in bars.
What's next, no f**king in bars?
Sᴇx ɪɴ ᴛʜᴇ Cɪᴛʏ

Tʜɪs ɪs ᴀ ʜɪɢʜʟʏ sɪɢɴɪꜰɪᴄᴀɴᴛ and often underestimated component to sexual relationships. This not only involves how a sexual encounter begins, but also involves how sexual advances are made.

Spontaneous refers to something occurring as a result of sudden impulse and without apparent premeditation. Thus, "Let's have sex" or Do you want to have sex?" is considered spontaneous. Suddenly caressing or undressing your spouse would be considered a spontaneous sexual advance.

Saying "Let's have sex tonight" is planning sex. Saying "let's have sex after the kids go to bed" is also planning. Saying "Do you want to have a romantic evening?" is sometimes code for planning sex.

Saying "How about if I put the kids to bed and we fool around later?" is also planning sex.

Planning sex doesn't mean clunky statements such as "Let's have sex at 7:14pm."

Clicking off the TV remote and saying "Do you want to fool around?" does not involve any seduction—which is perfectly okay. But not always. After all, what's the chance that you are both in the mood for sex at exactly the same moment?

It's not unusual that many married people—especially as they get older—want to first *get into the mood* for sex. Accordingly, caressing and kissing doesn't automatically put a person in the mood. Some people just don't click into the mood like a light-switch when invited to have sex. But they *can* get in the mood.

Some people want to brush their teeth first. Or shower first. Or they need time to clear their mind from their day's work or kids issues. They can't just jump into sex.

A little bit of planning with sex can go a very long way toward an easy and very enjoyable sexual relationship.

CHAPTER 46

Sex Drive & Functioning

—ᄿᄿᄾ—

I admit, I have a tremendous sex drive.
My boyfriend lives forty miles away.
PHYLLIS DILLER

I once made love for an hour and fifteen minutes,
but it was the night the clocks were set ahead.
GARRY SHANDLING

You know that look women get
when they want sex?
Me neither.
DREW CAREY

*The difference between hot, sweaty, jungle sex
and circus sex is that no one else should be home
when you're having circus sex.*

?

*My wife wants sex in the back of the car,
and she wants me to drive.*
RODNEY DANGERFIELD

THERE ARE NUMEROUS PHYSICAL, MEDICAL, relationship and psychological factors which affect male and female sex drive. You can maintain an easy sexual relationship if you are familiar with some basic factors.

The factors which have a *positive* effect on sex drive in a marriage include:

- overall good health.
- good cardiovascular health.
- reasonable amounts of exercise.
- being a nonsmoker
- good sleep habits.
- good hormonal functioning.
- overall good marriage.
- the ability to talk about sex.
- the ability to make sexual suggestions.
- the sexual relationship is enjoyable.

- compatible sex drives.
- being psychologically healthy.
- no alcohol or drug abuse.
- no fear of STDs.
- no fear of pregnancy.
- compatible sexual preferences.
- compatible preferences for contraception.
- easy contraception.
- good grooming and hygiene.

The following common factors which *suppress* sex drive include:
- depression.
- anger in general.
- anger at your spouse.
- frustration with a spouse who is chronically angry.
- shame.
- fear of shame and embarrassment.
- fear of failure.
- poor/emotionally painful body image.
- fear of inadequate sexual functioning.
- prior history of sexual trauma.
- hormone deficiencies and imbalances.
- antidepressant medications.
- blood pressure medications (and various other medications).
- various diseases.
- cardiovascular illness.
- fear of pregnancy.
- fear of STDs.

- ❋ fear of genital pain.
- ❋ chronic, non-genital physical pain.
- ❋ mental or physical fatigue.
- ❋ *being too relaxed to have sex.
- ❋ *loss of sexual attraction.
- ❋ *poor grooming and hygiene.

To the common complaint of *lack of time* due to work and children, the bottom line is whether you want to make time for sex.

Babies, children, teenagers, visitors, or grandparents in the house can certainly interfere with arranging sexual encounters. But sex doesn't have to automatically require either spontaneity or elaborate planning. And sex doesn't require two hours.

A little bit of scheduling, enthusiasm, and lightheartedness can help couples to find a little time to lock their bedroom door and have some sexual intimacy.

Teach your kids when they're young that sometimes you lock your bedroom door for short periods.

Keep your cats and dogs out of your bed during sexual encounters.

We all seem to have a basic awareness that mental or physical fatigue can interfere with sex drive. But what few people are aware of is that a person can become too *relaxed* for sex.

For example, when a person comes home from work and goes through a bunch of chores, plus dinner, and then lays down to watch TV, s/he is likely to become very relaxed—physically and mentally. The combination of being tired and overly relaxed suppresses sex drive.

One needs energy for sex—both mentally and physically. So if you're hoping to have sex, consider *not* laying down on the couch for hours.

The Internet provides instant information about what could be causing abnormally low or absent sex drive. Blogs and dopey, pseudo-informative (advertisement) websites provide little help, if not distorted, information. Look for informative and professional websites that address your medical issues and medications as possible interfering factors.

Many people (mostly husbands) think there's something wrong with their spouses (mostly wives) if they don't make sexual advances. Here's a good rule—if a wife can get aroused during sex, enjoy the intimacy and sex, and even have orgasms, don't make a big deal that she doesn't make sexual advances.

If she doesn't make advances, feels no drive either for romantic affection, sex, or orgasms, and has no sexual desire for her husband—then something is obviously wrong—either physiologically and/or psychologically, including the possibility of major marital problems.

Recent research has shown that *a significant percentage of married woman don't get into the mood for sex until the sex has already begun.*

To the issue of what is abnormally *high* sex drive, note that sexuality experts disagree whether there is such a condition as sex addiction. The term "sex addiction" has been around for several decades, along with other "addictions" such as food addiction, love addiction, relationship addiction, work addiction and shopping addiction.

Accordingly, there are 12 step recovery programs for these addictions just about everywhere. These terms are used by some therapists and lots of non-therapists.

Note that these so-called addictions are not actual diagnoses. Sex addiction terminology has been used to explain excessive masturbation, excessive viewing of sex websites, marital infidelity, deviant sexual desires, and people with a very high desire for sex in their marriage.

The definition of "excessive" is uncontrolled, unrestrained, unreasonable, overindulgent. But excessive doesn't mean addiction. A person can have sexual obsessions, sexual compulsions, or be obsessive-compulsive about sex in all kinds of ways within the marriage or outside the marriage—any and all of which may be severely problematic.

So, the issue is: when is excessive sexual behavior a problem or a disorder?

Factor number one involves assessing whether you and/or your spouse are distressed about your sexual behavior or sexual desires. Is the behavior illegal? Have you lied to and betrayed your spouse? Is it interfering with your work? Have you been fired from your job? Do you keep promising to stop, but don't? Is your behavior hurting your spouse or other people? Have you spent money on sex outside the marriage? Do you spend hours at a time viewing sexually explicit websites? Are your sexual habits interfering with the sexual relationship in your marriage?

If you and your spouse are upset and overwhelmed with your sex drive and behavior, and conversations are not alleviating the conflict, you both need to consult with a sexuality specialist. The specialist needs to be skilled and objective in helping you to resolve these very serious problems.

Finally, what could be more common than two people with healthy but different sex drives? Of course this can lead to conflict and problems. You can get angry for having sex or not having sex. If you want a good marriage, this is not a part of your marriage to be stubborn or rigid. You have to figure out *together* how to bridge the gap in your sexual desires. Otherwise, overt and covert resentments will erode your relationship.

A husband with no sex drive is extremely perplexing to the loving wife who wants a sexual relationship. It is often the case that there are no physical causes, secret taboo desires, or infidelities of any kind. It is painfully personalized by a loving wife when her husband has no sexual interest in her.

Interestingly, there's a pattern of a common difference between men and women: *A husband wants his wife to want sex. A wife wants her husband to want* her *for sex.*

Overall, it takes a considerable amount of time and consultations to pinpoint what the problems are for husbands with no sex drive. In many cases, the culprit is some combination of serious anger and resentments in the marriage.

Other aspects of sexual functioning include arousal and orgasm. Men may have problems with: obtaining erections or not maintaining erections (sometimes referred to as losing erections). Having inconsistencies with maintaining erections is not necessarily a problem as long as erections can be re-obtained without much effort.

Orgasm problems in men include premature orgasm and inhibited orgasm, also known as delayed ejaculation.

Women may have problems with inhibited arousal and inhibited orgasm, also known as female orgasmic disorder.

Typically, premature orgasm is not due to physical or deep-seated psychological problems. Arousal problems in both men and women can be due to a wide variety of physical, psychological and relationship problems, some of which can be very deep seated.

Inhibited orgasm in both men and women may also be due to physical and/or psychological factors and problems. There is a variety of types of inhibited orgasm ranging from people who have never had an orgasm to those who need extreme amounts of stimulation to reach orgasm. Get it checked out; it's a very treatable problem.

The above problems are typically very upsetting for both partners. Of concern also is that when a problem is not getting resolved, there is a domino effect leading to more problems, eventually leading to a loss of interest in sex and/or an avoidance of sex. This problem then dominoes to outside the bedroom in which couples refrain from affection and general sexual playfulness.

What definitely matters to a spouse is whether the one with the problem is taking assertive steps to get the problem evaluated and treated. Good faith efforts to address sexual problems are very important. It's one thing to have a problem; it's a whole other thing to not address it.

We now live in an era in which there is so much useful information and so much nonsensical information available to the public about sex. The good thing to know is that if your physician does not give you helpful information or concludes that your problem does not have a physical cause, you can likely find a sexuality professional who ideally can help you.

CHAPTER 47

Vaginal & Other Sexual Pain

—⁓⁓—

RULE OF THUMB: SEXUAL ACTIVITY should not hurt—physically or emotionally. When sex hurts, it is difficult and unappealing. This chapter gets rather medical because the information can help you with understanding the causes of sexual pain and also help your consultations with HCPs to be more productive.

Vaginal pain is the most common type of sexual pain. Women and men may experience pain with arousal and orgasm. Men may experience pain with ejaculation.

Vaginal pain is common and confusing. Both women and men often don't know what to make of it and don't know what to do about it. If sexual activity is painful, the desire for sex diminishes. Plus, the dominoes will continue to painfully fall emotionally, both in and out of the bedroom.

There are physical and psychological causes to the variety of types of vaginal pain. Types of pain include: irritation, burning, friction, pressure, stabbing or aching.

Vaginal pain can be due to: insufficient lubrication; aggressive thrusting; hormone imbalances; hemorrhoids; UTI (urinary tract infection); congenital abnormality; and herpes. Pain can also be caused by: medications; injury; birth control pills; allergic reactions; infections; personal care products; chemotherapy; and vaginal tissue problems such as dermatitis.

Vaginal pain can sometimes be etiologically traced to sexual trauma such as incest, childhood sex abuse, rape and any other type of sexual trauma.

Psychological and marital problems can cause both a loss of sexual desire and difficulties with arousal. Both contribute to difficulties with lubrication. Such problems include: chronic stress; severe anxiety; depression; extreme self-consciousness; history of sexual trauma; marital conflicts; and anger. Lack of and/or inadequate physical and psychological stimulation are leading causes of non-arousal.

Dysparuenia refers to chronically painful intercourse—whether due to physical or psychophysiological causes. Although genital pain problems occur in men, it is much more common in women.

Vaginismus is a condition involving involuntary spasms of the muscles of the vagina. Penetration can either be extremely difficult or virtually impossible. Medical exams may also be extremely difficult. Even the use of tampons is painful and not possible.

Vulvar vestibulitis (also known as vestibulodynia) is an inflammatory condition which refers to pain in the vestibular area (entry area) of the vagina and in the area between the perineum and labia. This condition includes severe pain upon touch or attempted vaginal entry.

Vulvodynia refers to a chronic vulvar pain condition. The pain can be be constant or inconsistent. The pain may be at the entrance of the vagina or in the labia and may involve stinging, burning or sharp pain. The pain can occur during or after sex.

Vulvodynia is diagnosed by a woman's complaints of pain. It can sometimes be diagnosed by pain reactions to slight touch on areas outside the vagina.

Atrophic vaginitis is not uncommon in postmenopausal women and is attributed to low estrogen.

Interstitial cystitis is characterized by bladder pain, urinary urgency and sexual pain. Painful orgasms may be caused also.

Endometriosis is a common cause of pelvic and sexual pain in women. Common symptoms of endometriosis include painful menstrual cycles and chronic lower abdominal and back pain.

Pelvic Floor Hypertonus involves spasm of the muscles of the female pelvic floor causing pelvic pain and dyspareunia.

Male Dyspareunia also has common causes. Pain occurring while obtaining an erection may be associated with: inflammation of the foreskin; trauma to the penis; infections; genital allergies; or Peyronie's disease. The most common causes of pain during male ejaculation are prostatitis and urethritis.

Finally, there is small percentage of people who experience painful orgasms. A small percentage of men experience painful ejaculations. These problems may be caused by psychological factors, blockages, STD's, nerve damage, pelvic surgery, certain medications, topical contraceptives or cancer.

If your gynecologist, urologist, endocrinologist, or PCP concludes that your pain does not have a physical/medical cause, they should be able to refer you to a sex therapy professional.

CHAPTER 48

Recreational Drugs & Sex

—⟋⟍⟍⟋—

A woman drove me to drink,
and I never had a chance to thank her.
W.C. FIELDS

The reason champagne is sexy
to a woman is because
the bubbles go to the vagina.
?

Erection Medications

Viagra, Levitra and Cialis are legal recreational drugs. These drugs have made sex enjoyable for countless men and their sexual partners.

Not only do these drugs help men to maintain good erections, but they've allowed men to feel sexier and more confident. These effects have facilitated their partners to have more enjoyable sexual encounters.

No matter how you look at it, these drugs have made sex *easier.*

The common mistakes men make with these drugs include: not waiting long enough after eating before taking it; not waiting long enough after taking it to be sexual; expecting the drug itself to cause an erection; expecting to not need sexual stimulation to get an erection; taking too small a dose; and drinking excessive alcohol.

I almost always recommend that a man first try one of these drugs with masturbation. It's best to know any unpleasant or intolerable side effects without a partner present. It's also best to know the physical signs that the medication is working (not just an erection) without a partner present.

Alcohol
Alcohol has been part of foreplay for centuries. Generally speaking, some beverages are sexier than others such as wine and sparkling wine. Some habits and rituals can feel sexy and inviting. Some beverages can be bloating and offensive. Not sexy.

Always remember: small amounts of alcohol can be disinhibiting and help a person to focus on pleasure. Too much alcohol causes sloppiness and sexual dysfunctions. Not sexy and also a health problem.

Marijuana
Some people have been using marijuana with sex for many years and they report that, in small doses, it works as a disinhibitor. Conversely, chronic marijuana consumption can cause loss of sex

drive and other sexual dysfunctions. It is also associated with a variety of other serious health and psychological problems.

Nutritional Supplements

There always seems to be a variety of vitamin shops, manufacturers and websites promoting all kinds of supplements to improve sexual desire and arousal in men and women. Yohimbine is derived from yohimbe tree bark and can create the illusion of sexual excitement in males. It is not recommended for females due to particular side effects. Ginseng and ginkgo are reportedly helpful for some men and women. Finally, Zestra may be helpful to some women for enhancement of sexual pleasure.

Other

Chronic use of amphetamines and cocaine is associated with sexual disorders including anorgasmia.

CHAPTER 49

Sex & Your Bedroom

—ʍ—

Women need a reason to have sex.
Men just need a place.
Billy Crystal

Your bedroom should be the perfect place for sleep, rest, comfort, relaxation, privacy and sex.

Your bedroom should not be a dumping ground for: piles of clean laundry, piles of dirty laundry, piles of old newspapers & magazines, or piles of old mail. Such piles are unpleasant distractions.

If you're a person who wants uninhibited sex, your bedroom is not the place for paintings and statues of religious icons *staring* at you in your bed while you're having sex.

If you're a person who wants uninhibited sex, your bedroom is also not the place for framed photos of your children, siblings, parents, and/or grandchildren *watching* you have sex.

If you enjoy feeling healthy and vibrant, don't line up your various medications on top of your dresser reminding you of your health problems.

Are your sheets stained? Are your blankets tattered? Maintain the attractiveness of your bedroom. It doesn't take much effort.

Your bedroom should be inviting, organized, appealing, and attractive. Bedroom aesthetics are important to both comfort and romantic rapport.

Music, lighting, and fragrances add enjoyable and erotic stimulation to a sexual experience.

The TV should not be on during sexual encounters even if it's 'on mute' except for, perhaps, x-rated shows. Weather reports, sports scores, traffic accidents, local burglaries, car insurance commercials, and international political chaos do not enhance sexual pleasure; they interfere with it.

If others are in the home, the door should be closed and, in most cases, *locked*. You can't be sexually uninhibited if you know your kids or house-guests can walk in on you while you are having sex.

You really don't want the lifelong memory of the look on their faces when they walked in on you in your favorite sexual position. They don't want that memory either.

CHAPTER 50

Orgasms Are Good For You

—∼∼—

*If all the men in the world had
an orgasm once a day,
there would be no wars.*

?

*I remember the first time I had sex.
I kept the receipt.*
GROUCHO MARX

*The only thing wrong with being an atheist
is that there's nobody to talk to during an orgasm.*

?

*If orgasms are a painkiller,
headaches are a bad excuse to not have sex.*

?

THERE ARE OVER 525,000 MINUTES in a year. A variety of sources indicate that male and female orgasms generally last about 10-20 seconds. One, ten second orgasm per week adds up to about forty seconds per month and a little over four minutes in a year.

It's interesting that some people don't even have four minutes a year experiencing one of the most enjoyable and healthful experiences they can possibly have.

Research has shown that higher rates of lifetime orgasms are associated with better health in terms of: cardiovascular functioning; less risk of prostate cancer; alleviation of arthritic pain; an asset to your immune system; longevity; mood enhancer; sleep enhancer; anti-inflammatory benefits; relaxation benefits; and promotion of affection.

Orgasms are also associated with relief and prevention of menstrual pain and endometriosis, in addition to less risk of breast cancer. Late pregnancy sexual activity may be associated with lowered risk of preterm delivery.

Yes, orgasms are good for you.

CHAPTER 51

Getting the Proper Medical Evaluation of a Sexual Problem

—◦◦◦—

We once went for sex counseling.
We were told to take hay-rides.
RICHARD LEWIS

GETTING THE PROPER EVALUATION AND treatment for any kind of sexual problem is not easy to find. Many professionals in health-care—both mental health practitioners and physicians—have neither the desire nor background to help you with sexual problems, including sexual dysfunctions.

Many health-care providers (HCPs) have not had the training in evaluating and treating sexual problems and disorders. Furthermore, many HCPs have personal difficulty in discussing sexuality.

Unfortunately, it is also common for HCPs to be dismissive to people with sexual concerns. HCPs can be quite judgmental about their patients based on their appearance, age, and health problems.

Another factor is that it takes considerable time to obtain the necessary specific information about problems and symptoms, and many HCPs are not motivated to spend so much time.

Unfortunately, many patients and their HCPs do a verbal dance of avoidance in not discussing sexuality questions and problems.

Many patients speak in code: "My sex drive isn't what it used to be." The HCP responds with "Well, you're getting older." or "You're under a lot of stress." And that's as far as it goes.

When I recommend to a patient that they need a medical evaluation of their sexual concerns, I advise that they be crystal clear and firm with their physician that something is very wrong.

Do not gloss over it. Get the physician's full attention. Don't be dismissed or trivialized. Get the evaluation done by a physician who will do a comprehensive work-up.

It can also help to do a little internet research on the common diagnostic tests for your particular problem.

Female HCPs are just as judgmental as male HCPs. Paradoxically, female HCPs, including nurses and physician assistants, can be quite anti-feminist in their beliefs by denying and dismissing the value of women's sexual pleasure.

I've heard many stories from women who were told by their female gynecology staff that it's perfectly okay to not have sex drive and just live with it. And so should their husbands.

Don't let your sexual pleasure be trivialized or dismissed!

CHAPTER 52

Getting the Proper Psychosexual Evaluation of a Sexual Problem

—ᴍ—

A PROPER EVALUATION NEEDS TO be done by a health care provider (HCP) with a specialty or sub-specialty in sexuality. There are a few professional societies who list members and certified therapists.

You should know the credentials of the therapist. Do you think you should be evaluated by a psychologist? Social worker? There are many uncertified, unlicensed and unqualified health-care providers. Be a sharp consumer. Ask questions. The evaluation and treatment of sexual concerns is not a specialty of most mental health clinicians.

An evaluation consists of interviews. Some therapists may ask you to fill out questionnaires. Don't hesitate to write down specific questions or provide written information at the initial consultation.

During the evaluation process, the following categories of concern should be addressed, regardless of your presenting sexual problem:

- Description of the problem.
- Attempts to resolve the problem.
- Additional sexual problems.
- Prior treatments for the problem.
- History of the problem in your marriage and prior relationships.
- Did the problem start suddenly or gradually.
- Your spouse's reactions to your problem.
- Other non-sexual marital problems.
- A thorough health/medical history.
- Medications.
- Hospitalization history.
- Any history of sexual trauma.
- Use of sexual enhancement drugs.
- Alcohol and recreational drug use.
- Cigarettes and caffeine consumption patterns.
- Sleep patterns and problems.
- Fatigue and lack of energy problems.
- Chronic pain problems of any kind.

- Genital pain of any kind.
- History of genital injuries.
- Urologic or gynecologic concerns.
- Depression or anxiety problems.
- History of individual and/or couples psychotherapy.
- Infidelity issues may or may not be addressed openly in the presence of both spouses.

By the end of the first consultation, your HCP should be able to give you at least tentative conclusions about your presenting problem and treatment possibilities. Prognosis issues should also be addressed. You may be advised to get particular medical evaluations.

You may be advised whether you need help by yourself and/or with your spouse. You should be able to ask some questions.

Overall, you want to leave with the initial impression that you are in the right place with the right HCP.

Part VI: Organizing Your Marriage & Lifestyle

—◆—

> *If you want things to change,*
> *things will have to change.*
> *If we want things to stay as they are,*
> *things will have to change.*
> LAMPEDUSA

LIFE ITSELF IS A SERIES of stages. Marriage also involves a series of stages. From dating to living together to pregnancy to a baby to children to teenagers…all the way to your retirement home or even a nursing home.

Part of the formula for having contentment in life is being able to harmoniously calibrate your priorities to the stage of life you are in. No matter what stage of life, your marriage should be the number one priority—at least some of the time. That means always being aware and sensitive to how you balance your priorities.

It's guaranteed that if you *never* put your relationship as the number one priority over driving your kids to a mall or mowing the lawn, your marriage will deteriorate. And then you will naively blame everything but yourselves for a painful marriage. So do your kids a favor and show them how to have an easy marriage and a good life. Be great role models to your kids.

It's pretty simple—if you want a really good marriage, put attention into it. And ideally it won't feel like *work*.

Regardless of who makes more money or who has a higher prestige job...regardless of how unique or special your parents thought you were...regardless of who works more hours...you should always be aware of having a lifestyle that makes both of you content with each other. Unless, of course, you got married to torture each other.

Okay, so this isn't the 1920's or the 1960s. And society continues to evolve incredibly fast in so many ways. The roles, demands and expectancies of men and women are complex. But marriage still involves two people living together, day after day and year after year.

A marriage needs attention, not work. Cooperation. Friendship. When sex is on your *to do* list, you know something is wrong.

Weekday Evenings

—⁕—

Life is about using the whole box of crayons.
?

Variety in your diet is health in your life.
Toni Sorenson

You know the standard routine: come home from work; put on old, comfortable clothes; check the mail; eat; drink; email; homework with kids; chores; TV (usually separate TV's); internet; sleep. Eating separately likely. Eating together not likely. Sex not likely. Reading, hobbies or exercising not likely.

Most kids and adults do not want to come home and talk about their day. If their day was stressful and they don't expect to get any satisfaction about talking about their day—they don't want to rehash it.

Don't cap your spouse's bad day by telling him/her what they did wrong and what they *should* have done. You weren't there and you weren't in their shoes. But you can empathize with their aggravation and you can talk about what they *could* have done. Just don't tell them what they *should* have done.

No matter how long a day you had, you can still carve out a little time from your weeknights to enjoy each other's company. It doesn't have to be for hours or even an hour. If you couldn't eat together because of schedules, you can at least be together for a little while.

Are the children getting to sleep when they should? Are you starting their bedtime routines early enough? Are they sleeping in your bed while you sleep in their beds (Kind of silly, isn't it?) Are you using the kids as an excuse to avoid each other?

Some couples find it pleasant to be in the same room together even if they're reading different books or looking at different electronics. Don't look for opportunities to hide from each other by being in separate rooms.

Do you really have to fall asleep on the couch every evening? Really? It's one thing to be comfortable; you deserve it. But it's another thing to have a tedious lifestyle.

CHAPTER 54

Weekends

—◊—

I really need a day between Saturday and Sunday.
?

No one looks back on their life and remembers
the nights they had plenty of sleep.
?

SOME COUPLES WAKE UP AGGRAVATED and *stay* aggravated, more so on their days off from work than on their workdays.

The problem is that the list of options and choices is endless for a day off: time with spouse, time with kids, time alone, time with hobbies, time with friends, chores, projects, shopping, errands and resting.

The list of what you have to do/want to do/should do/would like to do/need to do...is endless and stressful. No matter what you do, you might feel guilty, stressed and agitated that you should be doing something else.

The solution to this is two things: planning your days off and weekends in advance and achieving the right balance in your individual and joint priorities. If you refuse or forget to plan your weekend activities in the days before, at least do so right when you wake up. Take a couple of minutes and make a list together when you wake up.

Do not drop any bombs on weekend mornings that you have some elaborate plan for the day for both of you and expect your plan will automatically be accepted on the spur of the moment. Whether you want to play golf or paint the living room, it should be discussed before the weekend.

Do not wait until 5pm on Saturday to make dinner plans with friends or get restaurant reservations. Getting a baby-sitter should be decided during the week.

Overall, it's much nicer to wake up on a day-off feeling calm—even when you know it will be a busy day. Busy doesn't mean stressful.

Do your kids really need to have countless activities on your days off? You need to know where to draw the line that they can't have everything or that you have nothing more important to do than chauffeur them around.

Do you really need to sit through all your kids' sports practices? Do you really need to be there? Do you really need to be at every one of their games? Will they be traumatized later in life because you didn't attend their practices?

Try to have the perspective that the purpose of kids' sports is to have good exercise, learn sportsmanship, have a positive experience with competition and have fun.

Most parents ask their kids two questions after a game: "How'd you do?" and "Did you win?" Two questions about performance. Yet the most important question is "Did you have fun?"

Don't be the parent who screams at kids during sporting events. Sit back and enjoy the game. All too often, hysterical parents and frenzied coaches take the fun out of sports. Kids shouldn't be playing sports to impress you.

Overall, make selections and choices for your time off that feels worthwhile. Try to fit some time in with your spouse that is trouble-free, undemanding, natural and painless.

CHAPTER 55

Holidays & Special Occasions

—ɯɯ—

If love is blind, why is lingerie so popular?
?

There are exactly as many special occasions in life
as we choose to celebrate.
R. BRAULT

HOLIDAYS, ANNIVERSARIES, AND BIRTHDAYS OFTEN provide the best scheduled opportunities to romanticize and enjoy your relationship. Don't squander them.

These annual milestones are opportunities to have fun and enjoy each other. These are opportunities to go out of your way and pick out a gift—small or large—to show your love and appreciation for each other.

Some argue that they don't need a holiday to enjoy their relationship. True enough. Except people have a tendency not to make their relationship special on the vast majority of days in a year.

Don't always be practical with your gifts and celebrations. It feels good to feel special. Handing your spouse a mall gift card basically says, "I couldn't be bothered shopping for you."

Have fun and enjoy the handful of yearly opportunities to celebrate. Spend a little time planning and discussing the upcoming day.

Planning the details of how to spend a holiday and who to spend it with is a joint decision. I suggest you don't plan it first with your relatives. Plan it first with your spouse.

Sitting in traffic for hours on a holiday can certainly feel like work. Dealing with angry relatives who are offended you're not spending enough holiday time with them can feel like work. You and your spouse need to calmly discuss your own desires and the pressures from others.

If your partner loves gift wrapped packages and greeting cards—don't question it or complain. Don't politicize it and don't whine. It's so simple to do; just do it. Always try to make these days at least a little romantic. Don't dumb down your marriage with trivial biases against gift wrapping and greeting cards.

Fancy overpriced dinners on Valentine's Day aren't necessary for most couples. Plus, you could end up spending a fortune on a dull dinner. What matters is taking the opportunity to enjoy each other. You can have cheeseburgers and champagne at home—as long as it's something celebratory. And maybe a few laughs.

Don't be boring or cheap with sentiment. You don't have to spend a lot of money to show loving feelings.

If you label a new brown spot on your arm as a *freckle*, you forget about it. If you label the brown spot as *skin cancer*, you may become frantic. The point is that how you label experiences is what determines your emotional reactions. Try to enjoy the spirit of special occasions.

CHAPTER 56

Traveling & Vacations

—⟋⟋⟍—

*I'm getting tired of waking up
and not being at the beach.*
?

The first thing you pack is your sense of humor.
BRUCE FRIEDIN

*We didn't realize we were making memories.
We just knew we were having fun.*
?

VACATIONS ARE AN OPPORTUNITY FOR lighthearted new experiences, romance, seeing old friends, visiting relatives, and refreshing getaways from work and home. They're also an opportunity to relax at home and/or do projects at home.

Vacation planning may need considerable discussion and planning. Vacation time is precious and treat it like that. Be thoughtful with your planning regarding what would be easy with or without kids. In general, you don't want to return from a vacation feeling as if you need a vacation.

Vacation preferences may change as you get older. A hiking, winter tent camping vacation in your mid-20s obviously has a very different nature than a cruise, a Caribbean vacation or sightseeing in Paris.

Some people love to meticulously plan the details of a vacation while others derive no joy whatsoever from planning. This doesn't have to be a problem. If you're not a planner—don't be a complainer. If you don't enjoy planning a vacation, at least show good will and participate in the planning to some extent.

A successful vacation is partly defined by attention to detail. Good planning of travel arrangements can make a vacation flow smoothly.

Vacation issues often require compromise. Be a good sport, and don't be a martyr when you don't get your way.

Make sure you give yourselves plenty of extra time with travel arrangements. Organization and preparation make traveling a more effortless and enjoyable experience. Leisurely getting to an airport or hotel way ahead of time is not as problematic as getting there late with frayed nerves and agitation.

It's much more important not to spoil vacation time with tirades and tantrums than it is getting to an airport an extra hour earlier, having a coffee, doing some reading, and being calm and relaxed.

Finally, the fact is that things sometimes go wrong on a vacation. Lost reservations. Rain. Airport delays. Missed connections. Lost luggage. Unpleasant hotel room. Don't take out your frustration on each other. Be civil and as calm as possible to each other.

Part VII: Other Considerations

CHAPTER 57

Second Marriages

—ɯ—

A bride at her second marriage
does not wear a veil.
She wants to see what she is getting.
HELEN ROWLAND

SADLY, THERE IS PLENTY OF evidence that many people don't learn from their mistakes from one marriage to the next. They just keep making the same mistakes.

Such mistakes include the choices of whom to marry and the personal problems they bring to a marriage. Thus, they again end up in a difficult and problematic marriage.

Subsequent marriages may be even more complicated than first marriages because of: age, young children, adult children, step-children, angry step-children, angry former spouses, alienated former in-laws, financial child support, financial support to former spouses and the conflicts and pressures of combined families.

Children may resent the step-parent. The children may have rivalries. The step-parent may resent the step-children. Financial security may become a major issue.

Some people keep marrying people with drug problems, drinking problems and/or violence problems. Explaining this phenomenon is beyond the scope of this book.

The following suggestions apply to 2nd marriages:
- Make sure you are psychologically ready to date after your divorce. Don't jump into dating.
- If you still have significant loving feelings for your former spouse, it may not be a good idea to date.
- Know whether you are looking for: a relationship, some dating, or just sexual partners. Know what you're looking for.
- Don't casually fly into a second marriage based on romantic attraction. You need to make sure you are fully disengaged psychologically from your prior spouse and marriage.
- Consider getting psychotherapy after a divorce to learn about yourself. This may help you to avoid the same mistakes in any subsequent marriage.
- Investigate the pros and cons of a prenuptial contract.
- Keep in mind that sometimes you may react to your spouse based on your first marriage and its problems. Don't generalize from your prior spouse to your current spouse.

* Are you sure you can live harmoniously with your new spouse's children?
* Are you sure your new fiancée is over his/her last marriage?
* Don't get overwhelmed with enthusiasm if the sex is great (compared to the terrible sex in your prior marriage). It can distort your perception.

* Can you live with the spousal and child support payments that your prospective spouse has to pay out? How resentful will you be?
* Make sure the potential spouse is a good match for you and that you are not just marrying because of a fear of being alone.
* Parenting and discipline of young children and teenagers is a major issue. You and your prospective spouse need to carefully consider how you will handle this during marriage. Get professional help if there are indications of very conflicting attitudes about child-rearing.

CHAPTER 58

Crises & Major Stressors

—ᴍ—

Weeping is not the same thing as crying.
It takes your whole body to weep,
and when it's over,
you feel like you don't have
any bones left to hold you up.
SARAH OCKLER

That was the day my whole world went black.
Air looked black.
Sun looked black. I laid up in bed and
stared at the black walls of my house....
Took three months before I even
looked out the window, see the world still there.
I was surprised to see the world didn't stop.
KATHRYN STOCKETT

You never know how strong you are
until being strong is the only choice you have.

?

Stop all the clocks, cut off the telephone,
Prevent the dog from barking with a juicy bone.
Silence the pianos and with muffled drum
Bring out the coffin, let the mourners come.
Let aeroplanes circle moaning overhead
Scribbling on the sky the message He Is Dead.
Put crepe bows round the white
necks of the public doves,
Let the traffic policemen wear black cotton gloves.
He was my North, my South, my East and West.
My working week and my Sunday rest,
My noon, my midnight, my talk, my song;
I thought that love would last forever: I was wrong.
The stars are not wanted now: put out every one;
Pack up the moon and dismantle the sun;
Pour away the ocean and sweep up the wood.
For nothing now can ever come to any good.

W.H. Auden

* Death.
* Cancer.
* Degenerative disease.
* Infidelity.
* Car accidents.

- Kids on drugs.
- Infertility.
- Major surgery.
- Death of a child.
- Natural disasters.
- Job loss.
- Mortgage default.
- Financial crisis.
- Burglary.
- Skyrocketing home expenses.

NOTHING IS EVER EASY WITH the above sampler of crises and tragedies that can land like a ton of bricks on a marriage. In fact, the above crises can certainly squash almost any marriage into divorce.

With some crises, fault can be pointed accurately at one spouse. With other crises, neither is to blame. With some, both spouses share responsibility.

It's important to remember that similar to physical wounds, time does *not* heal all psychological wounds. What matters is the quality of the healing process that takes place over time.

In most, if not all of the above crises, a grieving process will occur. Grieving inherently involves disbelief, sadness, depression, and anger. Sometimes, lots of anger. Rage. Fury.

Some marriages will die an immediate death after a crisis. Some marriages will die a slow agonizing death. Some marriages will eventually return to their pre-crisis level of stability.

And, believe it or not, some marriages can become happier and healthier than ever, after a crisis. The reason for this is that other problems which were lurking in the background of a marriage may come to the forefront, all of which may get addressed and resolved in ways that hadn't been heretofore.

For the most part, a crisis/tragedy is a trauma. All types of trauma are different, yet similar in some ways. A person can be *traumatized,* yet not have a full blown case of Posttraumatic Stress Disorder (PTSD). Sexual crises are different from nonsexual crises and with complex ramifications.

One of my favorite *terms* is The Broken Shoelace Syndrome. When a person is struggling and coping with severe personal and family problems on a daily basis, s/he becomes increasingly exhausted emotionally and spiritually. Thus, on a day in which s/he goes to tie their shoelace and it breaks—it becomes an incredible indignity. This is the moment when a person snaps. Straw meets camel…The final straw. They've been managing the big things, but now this little shoelace causes a huge emotional reaction of exasperation and rage. Even furniture can get overturned.

Importantly, people need to go through life slower in some ways during and after a tragedy. Walk slower. Move slower. Think slower. Talk slower. Numbness.

I vividly remember the afternoon of 9-11, on a Long Island parkway. The cars were going about 20-30 mph; normally they'd be flying by at 55-65 mph or more.

Although there can be extreme demands to address aspects of the crisis, other daily life aspects may have to be postponed in order to maintain energy level, physically and psychologically. Some aspects need to be maintained for a sense of normalcy.

Marriage-wise, you may need to keep setting aside time to talk. Talking shouldn't be avoided.

Psychotherapy, marriage counseling, and support groups are all potential therapeutic options for coping, managing and healing from trauma. Opinions from professionals—whether therapists, physicians, clergy, lawyers or accountants can help.

Friends and relatives can either be helpful or stressful to you. You don't want extra stress from anyone who is forcing unsolicited advice on you. Medication for sleep, anxiety and depression can also help.

Crises can turn a household upside down. It's so important to be careful with what you say and how you say it—especially when you want to just scream, cry, rage and break things.

It's very important for your children not to hear certain things—whether they understand or don't understand what's being said. A primary reason for this recommendation is how children make interpretations from chaos. They can be highly confused, mistaken and traumatized by what you say or scream at each other.

CHAPTER 59

Gay Couples & Therapy

—m—

There's this illusion that homosexuals have sex and
heterosexuals fall in love.
That's completely untrue. Everybody
wants to be loved.
BOY GEORGE

If Liza Minnelli can marry two gay men,
why can't I marry one?
?

If you don't like gay marriage,
blame straight people.
They're the ones who have gay babies.
?

Gay marriage, or as I like to call it 'marriage.'
I had lunch this afternoon, not gay lunch.
I parked my car. I didn't gay park it.
?

I don't understand why people
are against gay marriage.
Their main argument is that it's tearing away
our social fabric.
You really think gays would do
anything to harm fabric?
DAVID HODOROWSKI

GAY COUPLES (I.E., SAME-SEX COUPLES) shouldn't assume that gay psychotherapists will automatically be more helpful, sensitive or skillful with them compared to straight therapists.

Likewise, straight couples shouldn't assume that a gay therapist doesn't have the proper insight and skills to help them.

Same sex couples encounter the same problems that straight couples have such as: communication problems, sexual problems, lack of romantic intimacy, family problems, parenting problems and anger problems.

Gender roles in some gay couples may not fit into the stereotype of straight couples. Therapists need to be sensitive to this.

There is a mythology that gay male couples should have sexually *open* marriages. Says who? This is a very dangerous belief. When a person is in love, they are naturally protective of the relationship. Sexually *open* marriages of any kind are like playing with fire. You are very likely to get burned.

It is perfectly reasonable to inquire whether the therapist has had clinical experience with gay couples. Feel free to ask the therapist if s/he has had either limited or extensive experience.

A therapist should have some background in sex discrimination, homophobia, internalized homophobia, health-care discrimination, family prejudices, alternative family structures, and children with same-sex parents.

Sociologist Pepper Schwartz coined the catchy term Lesbian Bed Death to describe the loss of a sexual relationship in lesbian couples. For those couples who want to resolve this problem, it starts with getting the proper consultations with health-care professionals.

Your therapist should ideally have a strong background in coming out issues—even if that is not the presenting problem you and your spouse have.

Your therapist should have a strong background in shame/pride-related psychological issues.

The therapist should also have some knowledge regarding local gay community resources and the gay world in general.

CHAPTER 60

Marriage & Couples Therapy

—⟋⟍⟍⟋—

Hope is not a plan.

?

Some apples don't fall far from the tree,
unless they've had therapy.

?

If one more therapist tells us to go home,
have a date night and light candles,
I'll never go to therapy again.
Is that the only advice they have?

?

TO THE QUESTION AT WHAT point should a couple start discussing getting professional help, there isn't a scientific answer. Couples have to address whether they've been openly trying to resolve their problems and to the degree of success or failure they've had. What is the degree of anger, pessimism, bitterness and feelings of helplessness?

An issue always lurking in the background is whether the unresolved problems are gradually eroding the love and happiness in the marriage.

Don't postpone professional help till you are ready for divorce. Many problems do not go away with time alone. In fact, they get worse.

<u>I recommend these guidelines:</u>
Your choice of a therapist is just as important as whether you actually decide to go for therapy.

The age, gender, and marital status of a therapist is not as important as you may think. What matters are their skills at understanding your specific problems, in addition to their ability in helping you resolve your problems.

Don't be naive to think that all female therapists understand women better than male therapists. Accordingly, many women prefer a male gynecologist instead of a female one.

Don't be naive to think that male therapists will automatically side with husbands and female therapists will side with women.

Don't be naive to think that the therapist's gender is automatically going to cause him/her to be more sophisticated or sensitive with particular sexuality issues and problems.

A gay therapist can help straight couples, and a straight therapist can help gay couples.

Don't be afraid to get a second opinion before your invest your time with any therapist.

The first appointment should be a satisfying experience. It's not a good start if you leave a first appointment with no sense of being understood or without any sense of direction of a treatment plan.

Don't go to marriage counseling to be told only what you want to hear. For the benefit of improving your marriage, you may hear that you are responsible for certain problems in the marriage.

In fact, when you get angry at the therapist, check yourself. Are you angry because: s/he isn't listening; you think s/he is siding with your spouse; or s/he has nothing valuable to offer.

Tell the therapist if you get angry. How the therapist responds may or may not alleviate your concerns.

Similar to the idea that you wouldn't want your heart problems treated by a foot doctor, your marital and/or sexual problems should be treated by a specialist.

Therapists can be judgmental, and they may have biases. They are fallible and can't possibly be one hundred percent objective. Be selective with your choice of therapist. Ask about their background, yet don't expect them to give you a full resume of their credentials.

When you're looking for opinions and advice from the therapist, don't be shy; ask for it. You are entitled to straight answers and professional opinions.

Therapy sessions shouldn't feel as if all that is happening is that you are having same arguments in the office as you do at home. However, some sessions can be quite painful. What matters is whether the pain is worth the help to your marriage. Painful shots of Novocain prevent the worse pain from root canal surgery.

There should be regular discussions about progress.

A rule of thumb with marital problems is that if you don't make any actual changes in your relationship, the problems will stay the same.

A major part of what some people have to learn in therapy is the discipline and patience of sitting down—calmly and respectfully—talking and listening about issues and problems.

There is no need to continue with a therapist if s/he is: falling asleep in your sessions; just stares at you and has nothing specific to say; and/or only seems to say "And how do you feel about that?"

Marital therapy involves work and a plan. Therapy should not primarily focus on *How was your week?*

With some problematic marriages, it is best if the couple work with separate therapists. With other marriages, it is best if they see the same therapist for separate sessions. With other marriages, it is best if there is a combination format of individual and together sessions. The format of three different therapists—two for separate therapy and one of marital therapy—is often too cumbersome. These options should be openly explored.

Regarding confidentiality and a potential conflict of interest, as long as there are no major secrets revealed to the therapist, and as long as there is no conflict of interest, the therapist can work with both spouses separately at times.

The most common marital problems leading to difficult, unhappy marriages and divorce include:

- lack of romantic love, intimacy and affection.
- alcohol/drug abuse.
- chronic inability to resolve conflicts respectfully and cooperatively.
- infidelity.
- chronic anger, arguments and disgust.
- flagrant incompatibility.
- sexual suffering.
- severe communication problems.

Happiness isn't something you experience;
it's something you remember.
OSCAR LEVANT

So by now, you've hopefully asked yourself if you and your spouse/ future spouse are easy to live with. Also, easy doesn't guarantee romantic love.

Of course, you don't have to be easy nor have an easy marriage. But remember: easy doesn't mean dull. If a couple enjoys drama and fireworks between them, so be it. Whatever makes you both happy.

There's no rule that says easy people make the best friends, best relatives or best spouses. But it's worthwhile to ask yourself whether you're easy to live with and whether your spouse is easy.

Can you *become* easy live with? That depends. If you're in a struggling marriage, it can help to carefully discuss whether it's the actual conflicts or your personalities that are the roadblock to a more harmonious marriage. Either way, it will hopefully help you to realize if there's potential for your marriage to become less conflict-ridden.

Some final reminders about having an easy marriage: Be flexible. Be open to conversation. Pay attention. Be cooperative with what makes your partner happy.

Learn patience. Have patience. Be patient. Don't become a patient.

Don't sacrifice romance. Don't neglect romance. Having children—babies or teenagers— is no excuse for a complete lack of romance. Have as much fun in your lives as reasonably as you can.

Be respectful. Be interesting. Enjoy life together.

Always control your temper. Words hurt. You can't take them back. Words can't be unheard. Again, exert patience. Take your time when you're angry. Don't raise your voices.

Maintain your appearance, grooming, and hygiene. Look good for each other. Pay attention.

Be affectionate. Be playful. Be complementary to each other.

Sit down and have respectful and patient discussions instead of half-baked conversations in the wrong place at the wrong time. Be a good listener. Take your time. Don't let problems linger.

Know when you need to get professional help.

Love is conditional. It is not unconditional. Don't expect to be loved if you continue to hurt your spouse.

Don't listen to the failures of burnt-out married or divorced people who tell you marriage is always work.

There is a beautiful Buddhist concept that serenity doesn't come from getting what you want, but rather wanting what you already have.

Best wishes.

C O D A

It's never too late to live happily ever after.

?

Paul McCartney once said—in so many words—that millions of little love songs have been written. The following lyrics from two songs just seemed to be a nice way to conclude this book. Kind of like what marriage should be about.

Don't go changing to try and please me.
You never let me down before.
I don't imagine you're too familiar.
And I don't see you anymore.
I wouldn't leave you in times of trouble.
We never could have come this far.
I took the good times, I'll take the bad times,
I'll take you just the way you are.
Don't go trying some new fashion,
Don't change the color of your hair.
You always have my unspoken passion,
Although I might not seem to care.
I don't want clever conversation.
I never want to work that hard.
I just want someone that I can talk to.
I want you just the way you are.
I said I love you, and that's forever.
And this I promise from the heart—
I could not love you any better.
I love you just the way you are.
BILLY JOEL

Love me tender.
Love me sweet. Never let me go.
You have made my life complete.
And I love you so.
Love me tender,
Love me true,
All my dreams fulfilled.
For my darling I love you,
And I always will.
Love me tender,
Love me long,
Take me to your heart.
For it's there that I belong,
And we'll never part.
Love me tender, love me dear.
Tell me you are mine.
I'll be yours through all the years,
till the end of time.
DARBY, PRESLEY & MATSON

ABOUT THE AUTHOR

Bruce Friedin, Ph.D. has held clinical psychology positions for well over 40 years. He has a doctorate in clinical psychology and two master's degrees in psychology. He also has two undergraduate degrees. He has held hospital and clinic positions, and he's been in private practice since 1982. He's had publications in scientific journals, as well as having provided interviews for a variety of magazines, newspapers, and radio and television shows. He has had a distinguished and specialized practice in marital and relationship problems in addition to all areas of sexuality.